AS IT HAPPENED

AS IT HAPPENED

Amazing Tell-Tales of Army Life

BRIG (RETD.) KANWALJIT SINGH

KALPAZ

As It Happened
Amazing Tell-Tales of Army Life

ISBN : 978-81-7835-953-3

Published in 2013 in India by
Kalpaz Publications
C-30, Satyawati Nagar,
Delhi - 110052
E-mail: kalpaz@hotmail.com

Laser Type Setting : Rajender Vashist, Delhi
Printed at : Chawla Offset Printers, Delhi

Dedicated

to my late parents

Dr. Mohan Singh

and

Sardarni Amar Kaur

Contents

Preface

Life has been full, experience vast, opportunity to learn unbounded, thanks to the most remarkable changes that have taken place, particularly in the last half century. The inventions and innovations have been galore. Computers, man landing on the Moon, unprecedented leaps in the study of the environment, enhanced communication systems, medical advances, understanding of the human cell and many more technical achievements and enormity of their magnitude were never spectacled earlier, and perhaps shall not be seen by any generation to come.

History, human nature and events, responses and reactions have helped create a heady cocktail of anecdotes, episodes and mini stories — woven chronologically to present an enjoyable volume.

I have done no research as such, hence no bibliography, and to resort to it just to enhance the authenticity of this book would be an atrocious thought for me. Also autobiography it is not, a bit of biography it may be, with substantial truth and correctness in the period, happenings and instances as I witnessed, experienced and perceived them.

I, however, have taken the liberty of changing the names of some characters and places, for obvious reasons. But I have chosen a common constant character and the best name that came to my mind was 'Kanwal'.

My earlier book "*Saragarhi* Battalion—Ashes to Glory" was a historical book of 4 *Sikh* (XXXVI—*Chatti)* which was released at its Centenary Celebrations in 1987 when

I was in command of that excellent outfit. Needless to say of my good fortune of having been commissioned in Saragarhi Battalion in 1962, and then command it as *'Chattisvan'* (36th) Commanding Officer on its Centenary.

The details available for the period from 1897 to 1962 were voluminous; hence summarizing them demanded a colossal effort which had started two years earlier, while I was on the staff. After 1962, I was an active member of the Unit, had been writing my own notes, and hence was fortunate to put them across authentically.

Being one of the leading Company Commander in Indo-Pak War 1965 to capture Brahmnabad and later Barki along Icchogil canal on road to Lahore; and establish a road block at Khemkaran, where I was taken a prisoner of war, gave me experiences of lifetime.

This experience was of immense value while again being one of the leading Company Commanders in Indo-Pak War 1971, launching four deliberate attacks capturing Naodapara at Boyra Salient, Chaugacha along River Kabadhak, Burinda at Jessore and finally Siramani-Shayamganj at Khulna, where the enemy surrendered immediately on establishment of road block by my Company, cutting off their major forces which were under attack from our Divisional forces.

The Unit was awarded Battle Honours of Barki and Siramani. History of 4 *Sikh* is of exemplary élan, steadfastness, valour, sacrifice and devotion to duty.

I also had the good luck to command 20 SIKH (Towering Twenty), an outstanding outfit, an Infantry Brigade along the Line of Control during insurgency, Regimental Centre and a Territorial Group. All this and some fine appointments in Staff and Instructional institutions gave ample opportunity to not only witness many events of significance but also contribute effectively in my humble way.

While writing 'As it Happened', I have kept in mind not to use military jargon so that all my readers can comprehend and enjoy the truth and spice.

I appreciate whole heartedly the interest taken by my elder brother Professor Ranjit Singh, a successful writer himself, who not only encouraged me to write, but later went through the script, correcting and suggesting improvements. My deepest thanks to Professor Upkar Singh, who acknowledged his earlier inability to improve my grammar when he used to teach me, more than half a century back: he thus worked laboriously to do the needful once again. I have no words to express my heartfelt gratitude to two beautiful young ladies, Namrata Gupta and Parul Chopra, who took extraordinary pains to improve the script in every way so as I could present it to my readers.

I must also acknowledge with gratitude my thanks to my wife Binnie, son Mandeep and his wife Kinnie, daughter Sonam and her husband Joaquim, for their whole-hearted support, encouragement and suggestions.

Last but not the least, I wish to convey my thanks to Kalpaz Publications who have contributed valuable suggestions to publishing the book.

Gurgaon **Brig (Retd.) Kanwaljit Singh**

1
Childhood Benevolence

A BORDER TOWN

Fazilka, located on the border with Pakistan, was established by a British known as Mr. Oliver in the name of Mian Mohd Fazil, from whom the area was purchased. *Fazil* is a Prussian word meaning 'a learned person'. Fazilka was unique in that though the city came into being way back, it was a right angled cross layout, its roads were straight and fairly broad, whether the main arteries or the *mohalla* streets. Fazilka also had a clock tower of an intrinsic design that was perhaps the tallest tower of that time. The town had a well laid-out sewer system even way back in 1850. It was one of the largest cotton growing *tehsils* in the country. The wool from entire Bikaner and that of erstwhile Punjab Bahawalpur was cleaned and baled into large bundles, to be transported to Bombay (Mumbai), from where it was shipped to Manchester in England for weaving into sheets of cloth. The move was from one end of the country in the North-West to the other in the South-West and then across the high seas.

The railway line to Bahawalpur in Pakistan lay abandoned, snapped by the Redcliff line in 1947. Suleimanki head works on Satlej, was with Pakistan, who had attacked India through it and captured area right up to the outskirts of Fazilka in 1965, and had designs to do the same again in 1971, but failed.

There were sand dunes all over. The Westerly winds used to be so severe that they transformed the sky into a black vista, visibility being reduced to a few yards with sand piercing into and settling on everywhere. The trees fell in dozens, electricity poles uprooted, roofs of weak hutments ripped off, clothes unless taken control of in time, flying off and not to be found. The rains were scarce. While the earthy smell of early shower was welcome, the subsequent stench created due to swollen dirty drains that overflowed into the houses, since not made for storm water, was disgusting.

The mighty Sutlej which once flowed close by had changed course, leaving a large horse-shoe area full of water which people named Baadha Lake, on the name of a small village on its banks. The Lake had deep waters of pale brown colour because of interwoven undergrowth and reeds along the banks or wherever there was some shallow water. During the rains, lotus abounded, creating a magnificent aura. There was a temple, '*Prachin Mandir*' in a high walled compound, a brick lined pathway to it and tall thick trees along it.

There were some country boats for the farmers to cross the lake to the island beyond or to catch fish, *rahu, sanghara* or eel. *Rahu* was tasty but full of thorns, *sanghara* had fewer thorns and eel had no taste as such. There was a large variety of birds – water crows, coots, egrets, kingfishers, cranes and humming birds. Frogs and toads of various sizes and water snakes reigned. The trees and bushes around were full of grey and black partridges, quails, parrots, nightingales, sparrows, crows, eagles, owls, kites, vultures, pigeons, doves, *mainas*, green pigeons, starlings and sand grouse. There were areas where the great rare Indian bustards were found. In winters came the migratory birds in thousands – the teals, dabchicks, pintails, geese and *bahmnis* (redheads). Porcupines, hare, deer, jackals, foxes and squirrels made up for the landed lore.

People lived in harmony. They were honest, innocent and believed in community living, not transgressing into others' beliefs, rituals or status. There were Hindus, Sikhs, Christians, Jats and Bishnois. The scheduled castes rarely asserted themselves.

There were all types of houses and huts. Jeeps and cars were very few and there were some tractors and two wheelers. Otherwise, the means of transportation were rickshaws, horse drawn *tongas*, donkey, bullock or camel pulled carts of different shapes and sizes. A few people kept horses. Donkey-pulled carts were popularly called '*Chevrolets*'.

Fazilka was a lovely place to live in, where *Malika-E-Tarranum* Noorjahan was brought up, singer Reshma lived in *Prem Gali* (Love Lane), and Mehdi Hassan received training in music.

With years, the prosperity has crept in rather slowly, being a border town it has seen two wars and there is always a lurking fear of another one. Landscape has been flattened, trees are lesser unless fruit grown. The lake has shrunk. Animals and birds are hardly any, with three or four varieties extinct. Migratory ducks come in far less a number and for fewer days .

The town has numerous cars, jeeps, tractors, buses, trucks and hundreds of two wheelers. There is awfully abundant merchandise. Hardly any wool and smaller cotton mounds, instead there are wheat and rice in the so called markets in the streets. Encroachments and increasing traffic has made people drive into whatever space available, making things chaotic and nonsensical. The area around clock tower is full of small time shops and fruit sellers. Pigs, stray cattle, dogs and crows are everywhere, as more filth is available from the materialistic living. There are fewer natural storms but more manmade fine dust and soot.

Progress has made people busier. Social living has become more to be seen among those counted and who matter. Competitive spirit has urged them to become more aggressive and unto themselves. Many well-to-do have moved their business to safer areas, leaving mere symbolic presence behind.

But those who had migrated from Kasur in Pakistan have brought the intricate craftsmanship of making the best *'tilla jutis'* (golden woven Punjabi shoes), which have been synonymous with Fazilka. The town is also famous for its peculiar mouth-watering sweet *'tosha'*–something like a dried *'rasgulla',* elongated looking like a thumb (man's; oof!).

Fazilka has prospered, changed from pristine ways to vulgar modernity.

Kanwal lived, was groomed and nurtured in this climate in a large joint family.

He remembers his childhood thus ....

ME OR YOU

Kala (Black) was no ordinary bull of Fazilka. Extremely healthy, broad forehead, round shining horns, protruding out alert-to-alarm ears, round eyes with a sadistic but piercing look, wide nostrils on a funnel like stretch from forehead, ending in a widened mouth, always chewing, keeping the nostrils wet, throwing thick white lace. The nostrils opened and closed with each massive heave from his broad chest. Strong stubby legs hauled a bulk in a steady threatening gait. The thick tail with dirty bushy hair moved to and fro. When he walked, people looked at him with awe, admiration, mirth, fear and respect — all in one.

After all, he belonged to a breed of known 'Sahiwal brownies' of Fazilka-Bahawalpur-Multan, large and meaning business. Alas! Fazilka and Bahawalpur are now in different countries.

The children hid away in streets or climbed the stairway outside the houses, huddled together and watching him in both fear and appreciation. The rickshaw pullers, cyclists, foot sluggers gave him a wide berth. The hawkers, particularly vegetable or fruit sellers offered something or the other, lest Kala should take a fancy to topple the complete cart, mince it into chips that even the best carpenters could not mend.

All gazed at his majesty's tread, some particularly of the fair sex watching shyly with hidden glances, his dark thick pouch with a sharp red spear protruding, dripping, dangling up and down, menacing and intriguing. People would throw water on his massive body in order to keep him cool and calm. After all, he had broken a couple of legs, an arm or two and ribs of three or four in the town, besides killing one.

No legal case could be processed against him since he belonged to the entire town. Complaints to the Municipal Committee had no effect.

Kala was no ordinary bull. He was the most dutiful and responsible. A cow needing a mate was never let off once revealed to him. That is apart from where he took fancy to. But that was rarest of the rare as he was always with the best - be it young, middle age or a bit old. He accomplished equally well with a virgin using his best of skill and experience.

Kala had become legendary. Cows covered by him looked fulsome, giving birth to healthy calves–best cows who gave plenty of milk or strong bulls for the fields or carts. People were satisfied and happy with the best bull in the area.

Kala was no ordinary bull. Till he had a match.

Chita (White), a 'nagauri' of Rajasthan-Haryana was no ordinary match. Pure white like milk, except black mouth, dark brown nostrils, brown eyes, black eye lashes, a few black hair on his tail and of course the red object protruding from a brown pouch. Enormous, magnificent and gleeful! He walked fast like a tiger on the prowl. He was huge like a hippopotamus, only a shade smaller than Kala, but beautiful like a thoroughbred Marwari stallion. However, people soon learnt of his shrewd, deliberate yet revengeful characteristics when they experienced his deeds.

Kala and Chita – pride of the town, rambling in the streets, around the clock tower, in the vegetable markets or outside the cow house. Very rarely they were together in the same area. In fact, it appeared that they had divided the town–Kala having his herm in urban area and Chitta more dominating towards the rural portions of the town towards Abohar and Bikaner. If there were those rare confrontations, they looked at each other with mixed feelings, flaring of the nostrils and occasional grunts depicted that they were measuring up each other.

Their enmity put the town in quandary as they charged at each other with the ferocity of two lions fighting for the pride, mates and domain. The thud of meeting of their foreheads, the grating sound of slashing horns, the rustle of the two scratching bodies, drumming of hoofs on the gravel or road and smashing of doors, windows, rickshaws or mere falling of one or both on the ground was a sight to see and remember. People tried their best to move them apart with water cannons, sticks and all sorts of luring tactics. No way. They fought ferociously for hours on. If briefly disengaged due to fatigue, or by the efforts of people, they would resume their duel as soon as they were close by. This carried on for over two years. People shouted, abused, clapped and betted as two menacing giants fought.

Till the day, Chita disappeared. Who or what took him away? There were tales *galore*.

But it left Kala bruised and limping, his one ear badly damaged, a horn dangling from his head. He began ageing.

Chita was no ordinary match to Kala.

Kala was no ordinary bull.

Nature made up for few means of entertainment and amusement for the people, and whatever was available was bountiful and thus gobbled up.

UNPREDICTABLE

Doctor Mohan Singh had a brush with a British Civil Surgeon during his first stint as the doctor-in-charge of a dispensary at Canal Colony Fazilka in 1943-46. Mohan Singh had been posted there from Ferozepur, where he had been specially selected to look after the problematic political prisoners in the district jail, who were part of the agitation and 'Dandi March' carried out by Mahatma Gandhi for India's freedom. The prisoners used to create self inflicted health problems and would not take treatment or would starve causing constant harassment to the British officers and Indian staff. With his uncanny ability, Mohan Singh convinced the political *'jamaat'* to eat, do exercise, and be healthy so that they could fulfill their dreams. The British bosses were highly satisfied.

While Mohan Singh was at Fazilka, a newly promoted British Civil Surgeon was posted at Ferozepur Civil Hospital. He was notorious for his ill treatment and harsh attitude towards the Indians. He was on inspection of hospitals in Fazilka. Mohan Singh had transformed the dispensary under his charge, as one of the most efficient model hospitals, where medicines were in abundance and treatment of patients superb. Patients thronged this dispensary rather than other hospitals.

The Surgeon reached the dispensary a couple of hours before the scheduled time. Mohan Singh had gone to see some needy patient, from where he returned an hour before the inspection. On arriving, he learnt from the Orderly that the Surgeon had already inspected most of the dispensary and was going through the documents. He was highly agitated over the absence of Mohan Singh, and was finding fault in everything. The Compounder was at the receiving end, unable to placate the Inspection Officer in English. Mohan Singh went to his house located in the rear of the dispensary.

The surgeon had seen the Doctor going to his house. He called for him and this ignominious conversation took place.

Surgeon: "So, you are the in-charge here. Why were you missing when I came?"

Mohan Singh: "Sir, firstly welcome to the dispensary. Since there was adequate time before your arrival, I had gone to attend to an emergency delivery case."

Surgeon: "Why didn't you come straight to the hospital, knowing that I am here, instead of going to your house?"

Mohan Singh: "Still there was enough time for the inspection and I had gone to wash up."

Surgeon: "I have learnt about your haughty attitude which is detestable. You need to be answerable for this kind of nonsensical and unacceptable attitude."

Mohan Singh deliberated for a reply, and said: "Sir, would you kindly like to see my dispensary and documentation etcetera and advise me if there are any aspects where I need to improve."

Several questions were asked. All were answered by Mohan Singh dexterously, in a polite, professional manner. It was clear to the surgeon that there was hardly anything he could find a fault in. Before leaving, he gave a piece of his mind to Mohan Singh, "You might have shrouded your weaknesses by your clever answers, but I am not satisfied. You need to improve your attitude towards patients. Your dispensary needs improvements which I have pointed out to your Compounder. You must behave when seniors come for inspection or visit; otherwise action may be taken against you that you shall remember."

Mohan Singh, respectfully pointing out: "Sir, I wish to submit something to you. But before that, please calm down and kindly ask me to sit down as I am the doctor-in-charge of this hospital."

Surgeon responded curtly: "Yes, Mohan Singh, sit down and let me know what is ailing you?"

Mohan Singh: "Sir, at my dispensary, all responsibilities are carried out as meticulously as possible. I am confident there would be no patient or people who are not satisfied with the medical treatment here; rather all will express full faith and appreciation. I take pride in mentioning that all my documents and records are kept as accurately as is desirable and possible. And now for the attitude. If you come at any time of the day or night for a surprise inspection, you are most welcome. I may be in the hospital or on some work elsewhere. If you give time, please adhere to it and you will never find me amiss. Even if delayed for some reason or the other I shall wait till told otherwise." After a pause, he continued: "My mannerism is exemplary. Just to point out some preconceived thought won't suffice as my hospital is doing a satisfactory job. Before I take the honour of requesting you for a cup of tea, please let me add that, as said by you about an action against me, anything desired may be done. I shall abide by the decision."

The Surgeon didn't say anything. He looked pensive and confused. Tea was presented, which he took quietly without touching any snacks. He was seen off by Mohan Singh to the car, the latter coming to attention out of respect, being an old soldier himself.

Mohan Singh expected an immediate posting.

Next day, he was handed over a telegram from the Surgeon that read: "I was extremely happy to inspect the dispensary at Canal Colony, Fazilka. Efficiency is excellent. Credit must go to the Doctor-in-Charge whose professional competency is of the highest standard. Best wishes."

Pragmatism surfaced through unpredictability; Mohan Singh heaved a sigh of relief.

A HOME

In hindsight, fingers were pointed at many people accusing them rightly of dividing a beautiful country into

India and Pakistan. Political ambitions, inflated egos, religious bigotry and mischief of the ruler, had been instrumental in wrecking the acceptability of each other by the two people. The largest migration in the annals of world history was affected, with loss of thousands of lives, unprecedented economic upheaval and total change of psyche. Doctor Mohan Singh was also uprooted from Manawala, District Shekhupura, now in Pakistan.

On reaching India, Doctor Mohan Singh was asked by the Punjab Medical Authorities where he would like to be posted. The partition had uprooted the entire family, his brothers and sisters had been thrown around, most of them dependent upon him, along with his six sons and two daughters. He had nothing but his medical degree, a highly supportive wife and a good name earned at Fazilka before his posting to Manawala.

He had been able to send his wife with children in a truck, arranged by a friend sending his own family to India, the moment they learnt partition was inevitable and riots had already set in. There was no time even to pick up a second pair of clothes. While the family travelled through burning Shekhupura, clatter of weapons shattering the stillness of eerie calm in Lahore, he himself was left behind, since in service. He moved on foot later with a '*kafila*' (caravan) of 300, himself armed with his German double bore, for protection along with a few other armed persons. After a prolonged worrisome search, fortunately, he was finally united with his family who had taken shelter in an abandoned Muslim house in Amritsar.

People of Fazilka welcomed him with open arms as he was an extremely popular '*nehri*' doctor whose instinctive expertise in medical treatment and empathy was legendary. Eminent citizens of the township, like Seth Shopat Lal, Sardar Thakur Singh, Babu Gokal Chand Vakil, Shri Munshi Ram Gilhotra, Kanwar Mohinder Singh Bedi, Shri Raja Ram and Rai Sahib Mukand Lal Ahuja assisted him to settle down.

To survive and make do financially, he asked his two elder sons to take up government jobs in whatever capacity. The eldest became an Overseer and the second one a Veterinary doctor, who eventually became Executive Engineer and Brigadier, respectively. Others in the family, taking cue from their patriarch, too, progressed and landed respectable assignments.

Mohan Singh was still short of money and thus resigned from service, to start his own practice. Hard work, dedication, highest professional integrity, strong surviving instincts that he had acquired, in his earlier service in the army at Bagdad and Basra, between the two world wars, stood him in good stead.

Besides doing extremely well in studies and always a topper, he was an excellent sportsman — football, cricket, swimming and riding were his favorites. He was an outstanding '*shikari*', worldly wise, a great story-teller, immaculately dressed and a gentleman to the core, hued in the British traditions of socializing with the best in a club, though for a very short time. His versatility in those days of scarce professionals in innumerable fields was always in demand.

His advancement from one-two room government apartments to a house on rent and then purchase of a semi-bricked house to a cemented one, along with other modern necessities, some agricultural land, was keeping up with his planned life. While his medical prowess reached phenomenal zenith, his guidance and advice was sought for forebodings in religious, political and social fibers.

Interestingly, he would repair his own scooter or car, electronic or water appliances and even knit '*moorahs*' (jute chairs), weave jute cots, Punjabi chords '*naras*' or make a colourful '*gohla*' (a bowl made of meshed paper and fuller earth). He was also fond of bridge, chess and poetry.

Mohan Singh died a highly respected man not only of Fazilka but of the entire district, the largest in India, at the age of 81 years, after a prolonged illness, serving the people he loved so much till his very last day. The day he died in 1982 was a full moon and it happened to be '*Makar Sakranti*'.

The news spread like wild fire. The people of the town and adjoining villages, in their love and reverence for him, closed all the markets voluntarily and swarmed into the town and the cremation ground. His mortal remains were taken on a decked up military truck, a military band in tow, through the main bazaar and the clock tower, where people showered rose petals on his body with moist eyes. His youngest son, Kanwal, was the last in the family to reach, just in time from Sikkim to perform the last rites.

A venerated, virtuous and versatile citizen thus left for his heavenly abode, leaving his large family in high positions of eminence that had now become an inseparable part of the town where they grew up and prospered. The people of the town named the street he lived in 'Doctor Mohan Singh Street'.

God blessed a home, Partition snatched it, efforts and aspirations fructified one, and destiny consecrated the ultimate.

HIS STORIES
Anecdotes by Doctor Mohan Singh

Competition

When he was sailing for Baghdad, Middle East, immediately after World War I, on much coaxing, he accepted a bet with a British officer (BO) of drinking as many cold drinks, as the latter's whisky pegs. He himself a non-drinker, thought the BO, at the most would be able to consume five or six large ones. The worthy Doctor could not cross nine, losing to the BO in number while the BO passed out. The Doctor had to look after a drunken BO. Next day, the sheepish BO presented a Shaffer pen to the Doctor, as according to him the bet was that he would be standing on his feet till the competition lasted.

(The fat yellow Shaffer with a golden nib, which writes thick letters since used for years, is now the prized possession of Mohan Singh's grandson.)

Drilled habits

They were stationed at Basra. Huge ice blocks were supplied, which were kept on the tables and being distributed to awaiting trucks. A number of people were working around, some were eating. One table, due to the weight of the ice block, became tilted in the loose sand. The ice block started sliding down. An Indian Non-Commissioned Officer, in charge of the outfit, in all seriousness shouted, "Halt".

All activities stopped except the ice block.

A swim

Mohan Singh decided to get out of the boat that he was travelling in, in Sutlej River. He instructed the boatman to keep it close to him as he wanted to swim across the river as was his desire each time he had the opportunity to do so. The current swept both downstream since the river had filled up a bit after the first monsoon. The boat reached the bank almost 300 meters downstream where Mohan Singh had landed. To his horror, while walking towards the boat, he saw some alligators basking in the sun, with their bellies up and mouths open, showing majestic teeth that sent a shiver down the spine. He made a circle from behind the bushes and boulders to reach the boat.

The boatman had also seen the alligators, so he took the boat a few meters further down; off loaded the other passengers, threw Mohan Singh's clothes outside, and rowed the boat back to the other end of the river. Mohan Singh was thrilled since he had saved two rupees that had to be given to the boatman, blissfully unaware that the clever boatman had already taken out two rupees from his pocket in front of other passengers.

Good old Lambretta

Confidentially, Mohan Singh used to narrate that once he was travelling on his scooter with his friend sitting on the pillion. Those days, lambretta had a fixed light which wouldn't move left or right along with the handle. Also, the spare wheel was placed on the side rather than behind the rear seat. The friend was sitting with both his legs on one side, lady like, and his hands under his armpits since the evening was cold.

As Mohan Singh turned a corner, he could not see a ditch because of the fixed light and thus the scooter jumped up a few meters ahead, and he spoke to the pillion rider. Got no response, he looked back and found his friend limping towards him, his turban tucked in his armpit as he tried to tie it up on his head. The friend told him that when the scooter had crossed the ditch, he had been thrown up like a ball and when he came down, the scooter had gone ahead and he landed on the road, but luckily fell across the wet ditch. They got onto the scooter again, the pillion rider this time sitting with one leg on each side, man like, and both his hands on Mohan Singh's shoulders.

Innocence Appreciated

Sardar Partap Singh Kairon, the Chief Minister of erstwhile Punjab was visiting Fazilka to his own community. After several discussions, his lunch was organized along with a dozen in the house of Doctor Mohan Singh. A typical 'punjabi' lunch was served, followed by a sweet dish of fruit custard. About a dozen and half plates were filled with custard, covered with silver foil (*vark*) applied with a sprinkling of cardamom seeds. Kairon appreciated the presentation and taste of the sweet dish. He was served a second time from a bowl, from which someone had already taken a helping. Kairon jokingly said, "I want with foil on it." To this, an eight-year-old Kanwal quipped: "But the foils are finished."

Kairon remarked, *"Ghar ka bhedi lanka dhaye,"* and handed Kanwal a ten-rupee note.

A FAMILY TREAT

They had gone for a picnic along a canal, close to their farmland. Monsoon had created utmost humidity. It was terribly hot, accentuated by frequent and prolonged electricity failures. Air conditioners were unheard of; desert coolers were of no use, only fans provided some solace. Water from the overflowing streets due to choked sewerage drains would enter verandas bringing lousy rats almost to the living room, swimming awkwardly or putting their snouts on some object yet not submerged.

Hence on a cloudy Sunday, the joint family of three generations, about seventeen of them, and another five from a very close friend's family, got together at the canal bank. The old lady had made *'tandoori missi rotis'* (*besan*-mixed oven-cooked breads), applied plenty of fresh butter, wrapped up in a thick cloth piece and put them in a colourful *'changer'* (a bowl made out of paper mache and *gachhi*) to keep these warm and soft. There were mangoes, the local ones to be sucked, and a mix of *'dushehris'* and *'langdas'*– to be cut and eaten. There was salad and plenty of *'lassi'* (butter milk), its taste enhanced with a dash of salt and pepper.

They all bathed and swam, joked, played and ate. There were competitions, one of them being who would finish the local mango the best, leaving no juice or flesh on it in stipulated time. It was quite amusing to see these people devouring the mangoes and licking the kernels, and wiping their dripping hands with their tongues. The results were announced, the first, second and third getting extra mangoes. Also there were duels of splashing water onto each other, other games and songs.

Tired and hungry, all pounced on the *'missi rotis'* laced with fresh butter, and sliced mangoes. Worthy *'Bhara ji'*, (elderly person respectfully called 'dear brother'), the professor of the local college, had taken off his thick glasses, and thus couldn't spot the tiny black things in the buttermilk. He took a couple of tumblers appreciating the taste of *'jeera'*.

The old lady realized that she had not put any *'jeera'*. She peeped into the bucket to find hundreds of ants in the buttermilk. Peals of laughter followed. Suddenly, the professor felt a gurgling in the stomach. Back to the town, he showed himself to a doctor, who gave some medicine and asked him to relax. But the professor kept complaining that he felt the ants were eating into his guts. An avowed non-drinker, innocently yet seriously, he asked the doctor, "Will whisky kill the ants, Doctor Sahib?" The doctor smiled and replied, "I don't know, but it will certainly kill your vow."

2

On the Roll

CLICKING

China had violated with impunity the *'Hindi-Chini Bhai-Bhai'* tenet, had stabbed in the back, attacked and humiliated the Indian forces in 1962 in the North-East Frontier Agency, now comprising Arunachal Pradesh, Meghalaya and Assam.

Kanwal was lucky to get commissioned in an elite Infantry Battalion which had just participated in an extremely gallant action at Walong and had withstood Chinese onslaught for 25 days, inflicting heavy casualties upon the enemy.

A farewell by his parents, relatives and friends from Fazilka was full of love, joy, pride interlaced with a streak of sadness. For Kanwal, the feeling of leaving all the dear ones was painful but the inspiration to confront the enemy and avenge the defeat soared his spirits.

At Delhi, he boarded a dirty red broad-guage train for his journey to Tinsukhia in Assam. For three days the train wobbled and hobbled, moved like a snail, letting out thick black smoke full of soot and coal pieces which hit like missiles onto the eyes. It stopped at every conceivable station, dotted by ill-clad, grumpy, melancholy people squatting about or sprawled around with blank looks. The country's poverty hit hard in the face.

Half the journey was in a meter-guage train which was rather a sad 'add on' to the earlier one. It rattled and woofed to negotiate even a slight gradient. The shattering sound made the animals look up in awe or run away, baboons and monkeys gaping with chattering sounds and birds flying away.

There was almost nothing available to eat anywhere except at a few large-town railway stations where the train invariably reached at odd hours. One could either starve or consume insipid food. Of course the '*besan-pinnies*' from home were a great consolation.

Whereas his senses reacted indifferently to such nuisance, his mind was to be with the 'bravest of brave' outfit of his Battalion which under the severest circumstances had shown its might to the Chinese in Battle of Walong.

IRONY OF FATE

AN OVERVIEW

(Sketches–1, 2 and 3 showing Indian Dispositions and Pattern of Enemy Attacks enclosed)

A flash signal for the move of 4 *Sikh* to North-East was received in September 1962, while the Unit was amidst celebrations of its Battle Honours Day, Saragarhi – a unique battle fought in Waziristan in 1897, where all 22 defenders died in defence of their post and all the combatants were awarded the highest gallantry awards for bravery, patriotism and sacrifice. Abundant money and land were given to the kin of gallant soldiers, with memorials raised at different places.

The Unit moved by train to Jorhat, then to Walong by air as a part of 11 Infantry Brigade, 2 Infantry Division. The aircraft, Otters, used to be of a small capacity; hence the Unit concentrated at the destination by October 21. 6 *Kumaon*, which was occupying forward screen positions along the McMahon line, had already, under pressure from the Chinese, moved back to Walong. 4 *Sikh* was deployed at a height ranging between 5000 to 8000 feet, on both

East and West of Lohit River, which as per assessment of that time was uncrossable. Ammunition, defence stores and rations, even water, had to be carried manually by troops from the base, from where it took six hours to reach the top.

While the Battalion was battling with the logistics and ship-shaping the defences, the Chinese launched their offensive across the McMahon line on October 20-21. By this time the troops of 4 *Sikh* who had reached the posts in the forefront, had occupied the under-developed defences. Each Company was some distance apart, hence not in mutual fire support; an undesirable situation, thus fought isolated battles. Chinese attacked in number, suffered heavy casualties and receded. The Commanding Officer still had not been able to visit his Companies, fighting bravely in front.

Meanwhile, at different stages of the battle, troops from other battalions, 2/8 GR, 3/3 GR and 4 *Dogra* were also inducted. Some troops occupied defences on both sides of the river, along with 4 *Sikh*, but mostly in its depth. Efforts of *Kumaonies* and *Gurkhas* to reinforce positions at places in the nick of time could not materialize because of enemy's presence or his effective fire. A counter attack by *Dogras* to retrieve a position did not succeed. Troops were moved around without success. The Brigade Commander had not been able to visit any of his Battalions in the forefront.

The information passed by the Commanders from the front about Chinese movements was received with disdain and misinterpreted. Even crucial information that the Chinese had crossed the Lohit in rubber boats was not believed.

Because of Chinese pressure and continuous attacks, ammunition consumption was voluminous, and replenishment inadequate. The men fought with tenacity, heroism and made supreme sacrifices, after inflicting heavy losses on the enemy. A soldier could not hold himself to his trench, leapt out, and killed eight before laying down his own life. A Non-Commissioned Officer, though wounded grievously, kept on firing a machine gun from behind a boulder, till his comrades moved into a more effective position. An Officer was seen firing from his sten gun with right hand, taking out grenadepins with left hand and teeth, and throwing on the enemy till he got a burst in his neck to die a chivalrous death. A Junior Commissioned Officer had picked up a light machine gun and firing, blazed into a Chinese patrol party who were trying to take up a dominating position. He himself succumbed to his injuries.

A Non-Commissioned Officer who had already killed a number of soldiers from the enemy camp, got wounded, walked back for eight hours, his intestines hanging out of his turban that he had tied on his stomach. Another Non-Commissioned Officer, got wounded in his shoulder, kept on fighting till he found all his colleagues dead and his ammunition finished. He moved back, took 37 days to reach the Unit, got lost in the jungles, with gangrene set in his wound at an advanced stage.

A non-combatant Non Commissioned Officer, a boot maker, outstanding hockey goal keeper, not only volunteered but motivated and organised other non-combatants to carry ammunition and mines to the needy posts for days, till he was ambushed by the enemy. He fought back, but was mortally wounded. He died, with the satisfaction of having completed the task he had undertaken – a rarest of the rare feats. Camaraderie was exemplary.

An Officer, Quarter-master of the Unit, with one Non-Commissioned Officer undertook to move forward through intense enemy fire to evacuate one wounded Company Commander, who had refused to be taken back by his men since mortally wounded. The Quarter-master picked up the wounded who was hit by another splinter that killed him. The Quarter-master himself wounded was taken a prisoner of war, while the soldier with him was killed.

After fighting a continuous battle for 25 days against the highly superior enemy, great wherewithal and strategy, but still inflicting hundreds of casualties on the adversary, ultimately the Unit lost ground. The Chinese named the position 'Tiger Mouth', and honoured the dead. Almost all those who died fighting were buried by the Chinese with due respect in the very trenches from where they fought, by putting outside an anklet, number disc or web equipment on a stick, for recognition later. The Chinese did not touch any valuables and buried the dead as best as possible in those difficult areas.

The humane act of the Chinese of honouring the Indian dead in the true traditions of chivalry and courtesy, and burying them in the trenches they fought from, was pointed by the Officiating Commanding Officer to the General Officer Commanding and the Brigade Commander when they later visited the site of battle on unilateral withdrawal by the Chinese. This was also confirmed by a Unit party under a Major, who had been given the task to go to all the positions, locate the bodies and conduct proper cremation. They found many decayed bodies in their trenches, riddled with bullets or shells, but their turbans intact, with stones and earth thrown on them.

Somehow, based on information from his staff and some others who had not fought enough, the Commander had already committed a lopsided view. And unfortunately, the wrong was backed by those in the chain being unaware of ground realities. The falsehood survived. This affected the relations with the Brigade Headquarters adversely. This was a case of 'injustice justified'.

In the battle, 82 soldiers had laid down their lives and 97 were wounded. Out of four Rifle Company Commanders, two had died and one wounded; Administration Company Commander was also wounded. Two wounded Officers along with some Junior Commissioned Officers and men were taken as prisoners of war by the Chinese. Only one Company Commander who survived had spent maximum time in the battle, and was the last to leave his position after many of his Company had died.

The enemy had been immensely punished in this sector. It was perhaps the only Unit in the Indian Army which had captured Chinese weapons. The Unit received numerous awards; no Battle Honour because of the overall debacle, but earned a lot of praise from the enemy, whose one distress signal dated November 2 said it all. The signal of frustration, which was intercepted and conveyed by the Brigade headquarters, was as follows;

'Very strong enemy defences hit near Walong. Request grant permission to withdraw.'

The reply was, 'No, you will carry out the entrusted task. Reinforcements being sent.'

The Chinese did exactly that. The reinforcements were in abundance. Many sub-unit level battles were fought. Hand to hand fights showed personal superiority of Indian soldiers in every way. But the superiority in number ultimately prevailed and the final bout of November 15-16 went in their favour. This was followed by the Chinese chasing the defeated of all the Battalions who fought and moved back as well as they could, hungry, lost, abandoned, and bruised in body and soul.

Sketch-1: SKETCH OF WALONG SHOWING DISPOSITION OF TROOPS ON 31 OCT. 1962

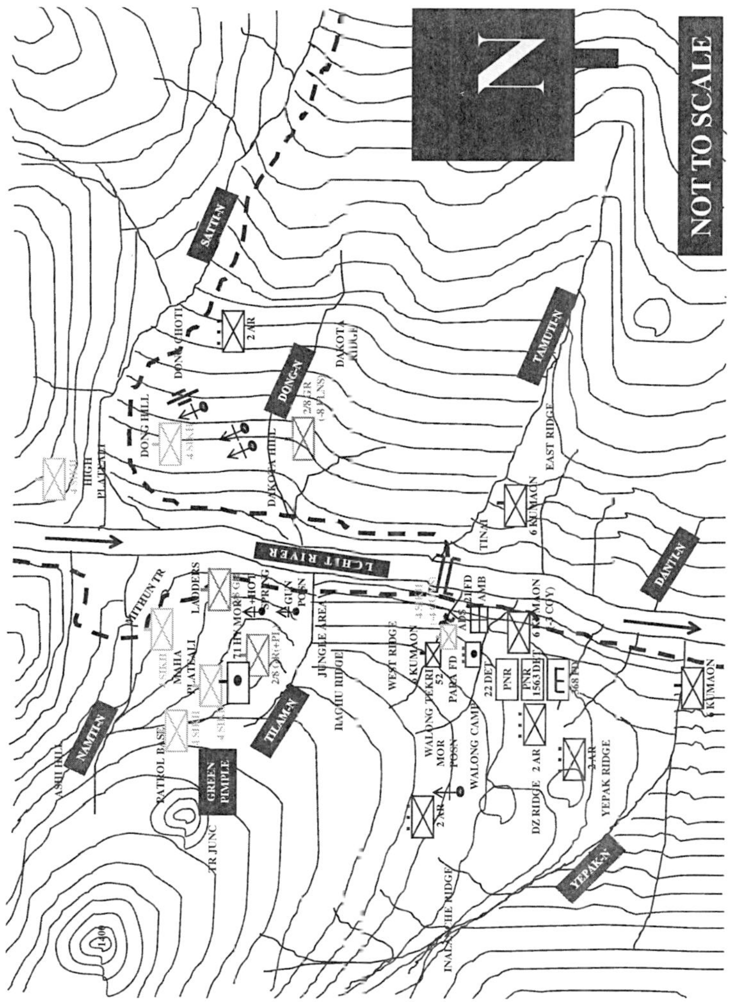

Sketch-2: SKETCH OF WALONG SHOWING DISPOSITION OF TROOPS ON 15 NOV. 1962

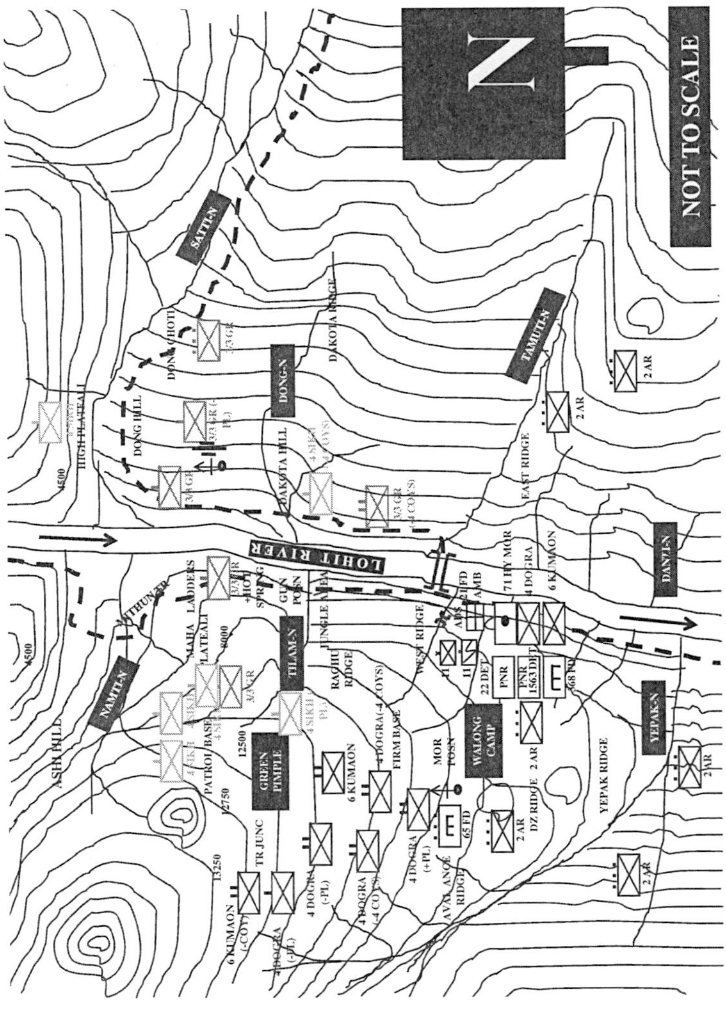

Sketch-3: PATTERN OF CHINESE ATTACK (15-16 NOV. 1962)

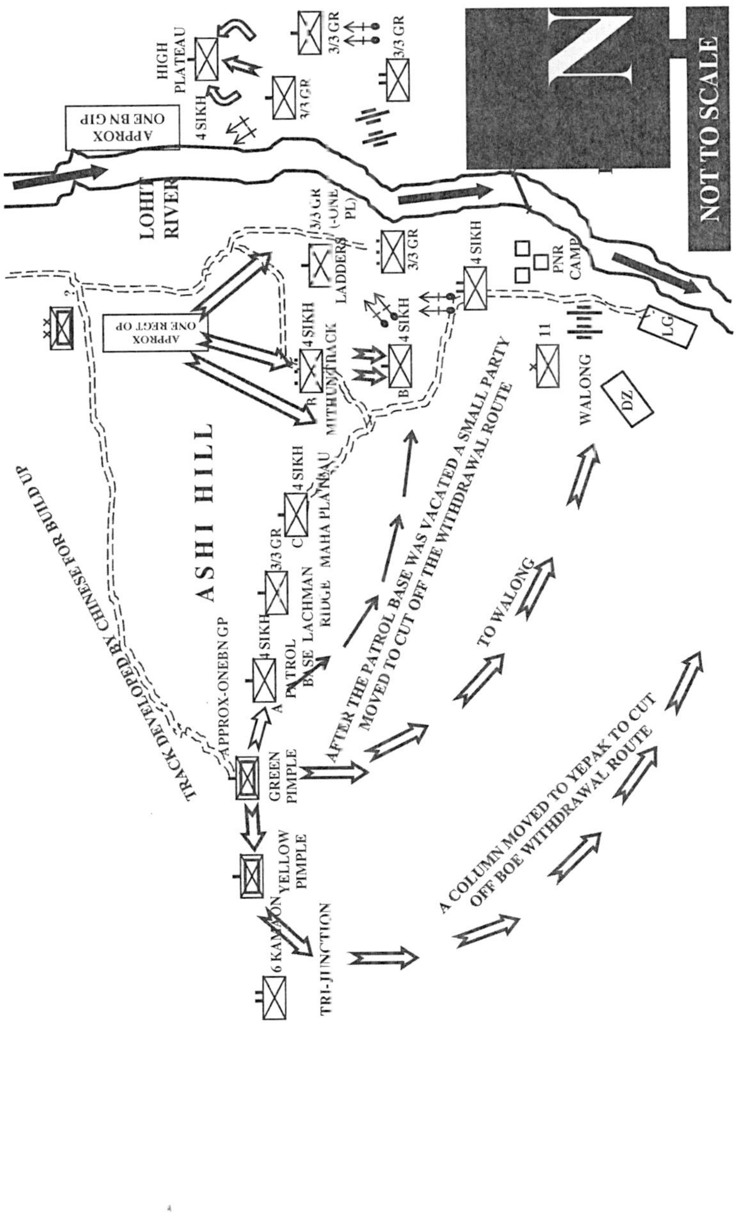

RECEPTION TO A NEW COMER

At Tinsukhia, in Tirap sub-division, Second Lieutenant RP Awasthi had come to receive the new comer. It was 5 pm and already getting dark with the December chill setting in. While getting into a medium sized truck called 'One ton', Awasthi with a bored look on his face, grinned and said: "Orders are that only one person can sit along with the driver but I allow you to sit with me in the front seat. Remember; do not mention it to anyone."

After a while, moving on the famous Stilwell road of Burma campaign of World War II, he asked Kanwal: "Do you drink?" Kanwal, very hesitatingly said, "Yes, I do but very little and seldom." Awasthi opened a one rupee and sixty *paise* worth of Hercules rum with great pomp of two slaps at the bottom and stylish forefinger and middle of the thumb applied with a push of the elbow to open the lid. What a journey through the towns with romantic names like Tinsukia, Digboi, Margherita, Ledo and Lekhapani! They had about three each by the time they reached the Unit at Lekhapani at 8 pm, the last rail station, on way to Jairampur border with Burma. Nobody was in the Officers' Mess which was made of bamboo and local tree stems. Two lamp lights were keeping the sitting room bright and warm. Awasthi said, "In the mess we do not drink rum, don't even mention it, and now let us have whisky Sohlan number one."

A thin dark man with snake like round shining eyes, tiny moustache, veins of hands and forearms puffed up, appeared on the scene with glittering white teeth, which looked rather prominent on the soaked out twitch-cheeked mug. "Kalu Ram, bring one small whisky for me and one for new sahib." Kalu Ram gave a pronounced grin to Kanwal and said in his torn soliloquy, "Sat Sri Akal Sahib, welcome to *Chhatti* XXXVI," with an air as if he owned the Unit. Kanwal felt rather proud.

They waited for hours for other officers to return from

Digboi Club where they had gone for a Christmas Bash. Kanwal learnt that 25th December was celebrated in the Army as much as, if not more than, *Baisakhi* or *Janamashtami*.

Past midnight, suddenly the light beams danced through the bamboo walls, the screeching sounds of stopping of two Willy jeeps pierced the quiet, and nine officers entered the mess. They had their revolvers dangling on their sides, mostly on the left. Kanwal now a bit 'glad' wondered why the revolvers on the left unless they were left-handers. Several Western cowboy books had taught him enough. Seeing the bunch he was elated that after all he had joined a cowboy outfit, which rode magnificent horses and shot rabbits running 25 yards away. A sudden thrill of bravado surged through his heart. All but two Sikhs removed their caps and hung them on the shorn branches of a tea plant. Blue eyed, the tallest, the most handsome and well built Anglo ordered, "Kalu Ram, one VAT 69 and glasses please." Then he looked towards vetern of 1962 War, a short Sikh Officer, shining eyes, through spotlessly clean glasses, heavy beard immaculately rolled up on the chin, with a wide grin peeping out of thick twirled up moustache, and said, "With your permission, Sir." Major Harbans Singh sharply responded to Major Ron Emery, "You have already given the order and now asking for my permission!"

Harbans, the Officiating Commanding Officer proffered a very steady hand to Kanwal, "Welcome Kaka, have a drink." VAT 69 vanished soon. Short, darkish and unassuming, normally to be missed out-kind, Major Abrahim did not let go of his 'privilege and honour' and proffered a John Haige to an already 'glad' gentry. A good amount of spirits came Kanwal's way to reach the legendary count of XXXVI (36) of XXXVI SIKH, but he failed at half the figure and was teetering to the appeasement of all. Tall, handsome, with a Rajput moustache, Major Shamsher Singh Manhas gestured to senior subaltern Lieutenant S S Duggal (Titch), who came to Kanwal and lightly admonished him for overdrinking and chattering.

Unsure if he had even taken snacks and food that night, Kanwal was guided by Second Lieutenant Amar Singh Sudan at 2 am or so to somewhere close by to a small tent, where he said, "Sir, I am proud to be in XXXVI and I am proud of you all–the tenacious cowboys. I appreciate you having seen me off to my tent. Keep it up. Good Night to you, sir." He mumbled some more boorish things about which he learnt next evening in the Mess, amid the loud guffaws of the well-natured 'toughies.'

THE METTLE

Suddenly, somebody shook up Kanwal with "Sat Sri Akal, Sahib, get ready for the long march. *'Pithu' (A pack weighing about 25 kg containing a soldier's stuff that he carries during operations)* is ready." Kanwal hardly had closed his eyes when the interruption disturbed him. He was still in the yesterday's uniform, half the buttons open, lying slantwise, quilt covering his legs and feet. After taking rather sweet tea, Sepoy Gurdev Singh 36 (*'Chatti'*-last two figures of his identity number), took him to a sack enclosure with a small pit and shovel besides loose soil and a rum bottle, full of water. A similar adjoining enclosure had a canvas bucket full of warm water. He quickly brushed, had a bath and moved to the tent, where he found his uniform and equipment and new jungle boots his size. By the time Kanwal came out of the tent, it had become quite bright even though it was actually 4.30 am, being east.

Soon he found himself standing in line on the left of Duggal, Awasthi and Sudan. The Subedar Major was giving report to Emery, the Adjutant on whose orders the officers moved in front of their Companies. Kanwal had been assigned to the 'A' Company as Company Officer. (A Company had about 120 men). Hence he marched to a spot right of the four Junior Commissioned Officers (JCOs), the Senior JCO and three Platoon Commanders. (A platoon had about 30 men).

Likewise, the Adjutant gave the report to the Second-in-Command, who marched in the other officers and then gave report to Harbans. Thereafter the Battalion moved in the Order of March given. The toughening exercise was a movement of about 22 kms, through bamboo jungles and tortuous hilly track which had become extremely slippery because of a light shower.

Some small thatched huts formed a village with a few scattered huts for field work. In these clean and open areas there were innocent faces of children and bright looking maids against the backdrop of tough looking men. Here and there, a bevy of local girls ferrying water or cutting long green grass for the cattle, proved to be a welcome distraction. The open areas were cut into fields of various sizes, primarily to suit the water flow and of course land ownerships. Mostly maize and corn were grown with a sprinkling of odd vegetables.

During the march, Kanwal went up and down his Company a number of times to check if all was well with his men. All this, left the men appreciating though not required, physical prowess of a nineteen-and-a-half year old slim, smiling and confident boy with a neatly-tied turban, whose beard had just started growing. Tea break at 10 am, lunch at 1 pm, afternoon tea at 3 pm, showed a strict regimentation. The afternoon tea was in a deep jungle, dark, sunlight filtering in slender shafts, rather reluctantly, due to the descending sun. Gurdev, the batman, heated up the lunch for Kanwal which was *'prathas'*, potatoes, eggs and pickle, and a small local banana.

Gurdev had put in eight years of essential colour service and had gone home as a reservist. Now he had been called back in the wake of the war. He had two daughters and a son. He had some land which was tilled by his elder brothers and being a joint family, all lived in the village in the same house harmoniously. Otherwise wives of four brothers quarrelled with one another, connived, backbit and thrashed out loudly cooking together, looking after animals or cleaning the house. Their fights used to be fiercer while putting cow dung cakes mixed with dried wheat husk on the walls outside the house. Their vocabulary was sharp like the fangs of a venomous snake whenever they had an encounter with the neighbours. However, children were dear to all. Husbands laughed it out, dreaming of an evening with country booze, mouthful of food with raw onion and chilies, and violent sex before snoring off.

Gurdev had one upper tooth in gold. His smile made him look handsome when he narrated the story of his mistress whom he used to meet behind an abandoned mosque. What a storyteller he was! Particularly, the naughty ones were narrated with full adjectives, with his gold tooth glittering.

The Battalion marched through thick bamboo groves, the stately trees, and a tea garden, then descended to the road. There was a 15-minute rest. Kanwal who had dozed off was suddenly woken up by thousands of butterflies – of all hues and colors. He looked around and saw a garden of pine apples, bananas and small oranges. The army of exotic butterflies seduced with the hum of their flaps, only to be interrupted by the noise of a truck full of labourers, going home. Men and women were drunk—singing and dancing.

On return, Gurdev expressed his satisfaction and appreciation of his new Sahib who was tough like a thoroughbred. The new sahib felt proud of his home town, where he had played football, and of course local games like *pithoo, guli danda, ghori ghurmas, ill kangra, lukan mitti, kabaddi, chicho-chich and khido-khundi*, all requiring good physique, tact, stamina and intelligence. (These sports were played as hotch potch Olympics where Kala and Chita amused one and all with their fights between themselves, and of course their amorous encounters with the deserving cows.)

BLABBER

To raise the morale of the men and to improve upon strained relationship with the higher Headquarters, two of the most impressive of their own kind Lieutenant Generals, one Colonel of the Regiment, a war veteran of World War

II and 1947 and 1965 Indo-Pak Wars, and the other a Maharaja, Honorary Colonel of the Regiment, along with many others, paid a visit to the Unit. Official formalities done, a party in the Officers' Mess was organized.

Apart from many army officers, some civilians of repute, including Indians and foreigners, were invited. They all came with their gorgeous wives from tea gardens and oil refineries. Their style of living and conduct had a class.

Second Lieutenant Bakshi, while talking to a young petite lady said in his typical Punjabi accent, "I admire the *'bay'* you *'libe' 'bhere'* snakes abound, particularly this story of a huge snake crossing the road in front of your car *'bhile'* coming here. Here *'bhere' 'bue'* are *'libing'* there are many, particularly one *'bery'* big near my tent *'bhich'* if you don't believe I can show you *'eben'* now." Harbans, who had heard this conversation, after a while teased Bakshi, "*Salia, saanu te kade dikhaya nahin*" (You boasting rascal, you have never shown one to us).

BITTER SWEET DRIVEL

The previous Commanding Officer was allegedly not up to the mark during the battle, so the Brigade Commander had sent him on leave followed by posting out. His then Second-in-Command who had displayed outstanding grit and fortitude during the major portion of the battle had been moved out on promotion just before the winning attack of the Chinese.

A Lieutenant Colonel from another Battalion was posted in. Somehow, he came with some misconceptions and thus took upon himself with a challenge; to shake up the Unit from its slumber as perceived by him. He ordered a rather tough workout for a month, notwithstanding the unpleasant feelings in the Unit of misunderstandings with the higher Headquarters, its achievements yet its sufferings. Some of his idiosyncrasies were childish and laughable. He became unpopular in no time.

On a Saturday, he decided to spend a night at one of the tea gardens with the manager and his family, thus he left in the evening for an hour and a half drive. So as others were not left behind, he gave instructions to officers for most of them to join next day for a picnic for which some other tea planters had also been invited. Most of the senior officers stayed back, others reaching the venue a little before time.

They found him, sitting in the lawn with his long hair and beard open, wearing a red and white striped sleeping suit and a borrowed blue gown, basking in the nice winter sun with a newspaper in hand. Smiling rather proudly, he said, "Bathroom was so lavish with all its fitments and toiletries that I could not resist a thorough bath." "No wonder" thought the officers as they noticed a Punjabi style large underwear hanging upright on a line dried up only partially.

After a while he returned from the bedroom to the living area, his trousers slightly wet just above the knees, where the lower portion of the underwear reached. He followed the gaze of his officers, sat down quickly with his hands upon the wet portions. He got up rather reluctantly each time someone came to meet, hastily to resume the seat till trousers dried up a bit, ultimately allowing him to move to the picnic spot.

He got his posting orders to move forthwith thus leaving a memorable one month's impact for only those who knew him. (The irony was his photograph was missing from Rogues' Gallery, since he refused to send the same).

LEECH

These slimy creatures were so detestable to look at. They could be long, one and half to three and half inches, thin or thick; black, brown, yellow or a mix. Soft bodied and light — they gave a feeling of a petal caressing glued to a person.

Anatomically, they had thirty four segments in their body, with six in front which helped in sucking blood. These leeches of Assam differed from those of freshwater, terrestrial or marines.

The bushy wet areas were full of them, they infested along the water bodies, streams or they thrived in bamboo groves. When people moved in a single file on a jungle track, first two or three persons were safe, thereafter others invariably found these creatures diving on to them from trees, catching on when rustling along bushes or from ground making their way through the eyes of the shoes. Unless a person came to know earlier, when full they dropped off into the clothes from behind the ears, neck, and armpit, or from between the fingers of the feet, leaving an itch at the place they sucked. When shoes were taken off, very often they used to be found full slightly red, or a dead one with blood all over.

Kanwal, during a defence exercise in 1963, with about 120 soldiers under him, was allotted a hillock which had thousands of leeches. While briefing the bosses he did make a point by giving geographical features, names as Leech Spur, Leech *'Pahari'*, *'Jok'* Valley, Leech knoll or *'Jok'* Saddle. At night, troops sprinkled mosquito oil or salt, and smokers spread tobacco all around. Still, by the morning, most had been bit.

The men removed them rather crudely, plucking them away, always finding blood oozing out for sometime thereafter, which caused prolonged itching. The advice was to insert spoon handle or a knife under the leech's belly in the rear and move it forward to remove the mouth slowly to restrict sucked blood back into the wound. This would stop bleeding instantaneously with lesser itching.

A tiger leech had its way that day. The army officers were out on a picnic along an enchanting stream. They had invited some civilians–Merchants, Holidays, Sehgals, Randhawas and a few others from Digboi, Margherita and Ledo. Ladies looked deadly in their swim suits.

Major Cooper who had taken plenty of beer and was in his swimming costume felt the nature's urge, went behind the '*kanat*' (curtain), which had been put up for gents 'greening the plants'. A striped leech suddenly dropped from a branch above onto his prick's knob and he squeaked "leech", swirled about rather violently, bringing down the '*kanat*', his nakedness pointing out at the bar-be-queue stand.

Some commotion and giggles later, the '*kanat*' was re-erected. Cooper switched over to neat whisky to shrivel nature's call.

3

Sunny Days

IMPUDENTLY VIRTUOUS

Due to the shortage of regular manpower, hundreds of reservists on active list had been recalled after the 1962 war. In those days soldiers had an active service of eight years, and seven years of reserve service, during which in emergency, they could be called back to join duty. Sepoy Gurdev Singh was one of them recalled to his Unit at Lekhapani. Since he had his namesakes in the Unit, he was always identified by Gurdev 36 (*chhatti)*, 36 being the last two digits of his Identity-disc number.

Gurdev was known for his notorious 'absent without leave', 'overstay leave' or for quarrelling with others, especially after taking booze. Thanks to daily issue of two ounces as medical advice in those areas, he managed extra, either from a non-drinker or tying up with someone not drinking due to some religious ritual or compulsion of duty.

It was amazing that in spite of those traits, he was selected as a reservist. Probably, it was his chivalrous and cheerful demeanour, positive and helpful attitude, excellence in '*bhangra*' and his rugged handsome Punjabi looks that won the day for him.

Kanwal did what the young officers often did of asking for the most difficult man to handle, to be provided as batman (helper or '*sahayak*'). His audacity bagged him Gurdev 36. The batman's job was as a buddy-in-arm to the officer, to assist him in every way in the upkeep of where he lived, to keep his uniforms, equipment and weapon ready, and numerous such other errands so as the officer was free to devote himself to other essential functions of the command.

The moment Gurdev was selected, his stature in the Company was enhanced. He managed to get a large '*basha*' (bamboo-hut) made for Kanwal with attached bathroom, cot, tables and chairs made from bamboo. His dedication was admired by all. He reduced his drinking to the fixed quota; after all he was then a responsible man.

One night, Kanwal returned along with other officers pretty late from a party at Digboi club. The moment he entered his *basha*, he found dim light of the lantern and Gurdev sleeping on his bed, mouth open, sprawled with his legs apart, arms outstretched, his '*khaki*' canvas shoes on his feet and turban slightly tilted.

Kanwal was gripped with a sudden rage which somehow subsided as quickly. He shouted Gurdev's name a few times but no response. Then he shook him up wildly to which Gurdev responded by taking off his shoes and placing them on the shoe-rack beside. Then he took off his turban and kept it on the shelf behind the bed, after all he knew all the places he had got made in the room. Both actions were done without opening his eyelids. He then turned to his side and started snoring.

Kanwal went out and asked the sentry to call Subedar Sahib who came in no time. He caught hold of Gurdev's collars, hauled him up throwing him on the ground, and gave him three or four slaps which brought him back to his senses. Gurdev quickly picked up his turban and shoes and ran out of the room as fast as he could.

Before Subedar's apology for his man having failed him could finish, Gurdev peeped in and said, "Sahib Ji, my mistake. Please have mercy on me." And he vanished from the scene. Gurdev could not be found in the lines that night. In the morning, with a neatly tied turban and rolled up beard, in a clean outfit, he came to Kanwal's *basha* with a hot cup of tea, "Sat Sri Akal Sahib. I have brought tea for you, Sir. But Sahib Ji, you should not keep liquor in your box and give the keys to me. Sir imagine, what would have happened if I had opened the second bottle too?"

FAITH

The Indian Army was transforming in weaponry, tactics and attitude. Lethargy had given way to activation on all fronts. All endeavour was directed to mental makeup, as the soldiers' morale was worst affected after the 1962 debacle. At lower levels, as per the policy, was to do maximum long range patrolling up to and along the line of control, covering the passes. This was done with triple purpose of familiarisation and domination of the area, thus attaining ascendency, instilling confidence among the civilian populace and toughening up of troops.

Patrols comprised 10-20 in strength and generally used to be out for 10-15 days. The troops had to be self-contained in every respect — weapons, ammunition, ration and arrangements for shelter. All carried approximately 40-50 kilogram of weight. To cover the distance average walking used to be 20 miles or so each day, on beaten paths or unbeaten animal tracks, tedious, narrow and dangerous, through jungles, valleys, *nullahs*, steep mountains and snow. Heavy communication equipment had to be carried along to report to parent Headquarters.

It needed tremendous stamina, courage and guts because many a time movement was through eerily quiet jungles, with graves of people or signs of soldiers having died there, who had done their best against heavy odds, but defeated and humiliated, moving back, wounded, scarcely clad, hungry and exhausted. They had been abandoned due to impervious follies of political masters, timid and ruptured higher military leadership and superior and treacherous enemy.

Despite all this, the soldiers were also a witness to the breathtaking beauty of the snow clad hills at dawn, day and dusk. Stunning waterfalls, fascinating precipitating streams of clear blue waters, gushing rivers, gorgeous thick green forests and the breeze, fauna and flora augmented with the natural innocence of beautiful people transported a person to a dreamland.

A Patrol under lanky Captain Balraj Bakshi, of about 15 personnel, was assigned a task for a 10 day sojourn. He was given an under trainee Second Lieutenant Mukerji, hailing from Calcutta, an intelligent handsome sportsman, humorous and clever. For three days the patrol moved smoothly with great enthusiasm.

On the fourth morning, because of fog the patrol started late, it rained enroute and thus a further delay was caused. All got tired soon. Dragging their feet, they climbed a hill, and then descended falling many a time on the slippery steep track to a ravishingly beautiful cascading rivulet. Though there were two hours to dusk and little more distance to their destination for that day, Subedar Darshan proposed to halt for the night.

A message was conveyed to the Headquarters that they had reached the designated place. The signaling wireless set thereafter was switched off. Balraj Bakshi was relaxing when he heard a Hindi song. He found the music from the signaling set which had been switched on by Darshan. Bakshi ordered Darshan to switch it off but Darshan refused blatantly. Bakshi himself went to the set and switched it off. He then went to his shelter which was nothing but a ground-sheet tied with a sturdy twig of a bush on one side and a dried up tree on the other. Some grass and his raincoat on it made his bed.

After a few minutes, the music started again. There was a heated argument between Bakshi and Darshan. Ultimately Bakshi picked up the battery and brought it to his shelter.

This affected the mood of the entire patrol which worsened because of the ongoing altercations between the two. The entire planned patrolling went haywire and they lost track completely by the sixth day.

On the seventh day, Muku found Bakshi, behind the boulders, with a picture of a Guru in front, his hands folded praying loudly, "God Almighty, please help me, bless me to find the way otherwise I will be ruined." Muku saluted Bakshi and said, "Sir, if you do not mind, please. Indian Military Academy has given us training, the Map Section has provided maps and God Almighty has given us brains. Let us use all these and find the way." As luck would have it, they found a tiny village and got help to move further on to their route.

But they had lost a good two days and would in no way be able to complete the task. They had to move back where they were the previous day, since they had strayed from the assigned route from there. Eventually, the patrol returned to the Headquarters in time to report that the task had been done successfully.

The faith in the achievement, esprit de corps, necessity of survival and a call of 'save our soul' had drowned the vulgarities of what should not have happened. Bakshi and Darshan patched up, men found new bonhomie; Bakshi's faith in God Almighty was refurbished. Mukerji's belief in the use of brains, map and training was reinforced.

ORCHIDS

Foothills of Arunachal were famous for more than 900 varieties of exotic orchids, always calling to remind femme fatale. It was where the Unit was stationed. In 1960s, the forests had not been ravaged by inexorable onslaught of commercialization and development. The vast variety of orchids could be seen in the scanty villages and lone huts along the roads or paths, as also in jungles during patrolling or military exercises.

The sight of these beauties drove the sight seers wild and nostalgic. The orchids with their enormous medicinal value, particularly for 'libido' as the name is derived from the Greek word 'orchis' meaning 'testicles', always got the adrenalin soaring. The North-East had the perfect climate for orchids that survived upon heavy rainfall, humidity and warm temperature.

Major Chand Ram, Second-in-Command, was crazy about flora and fauna. Whenever any long range patrol went out, he made it a point to tell the leader to look for something exotic and alluring–be it a bird, animal, plant, shrub or drift wood. Particularly, the sight of an orchid brought a surge of jubilation in him. He never excused anybody if that person brought a parasite by mistake.

Patrols were declared successful, if they brought something of his choice. Thus, there were choicest of flowers, orchids, rhododendron roots and driftwood not only in the Mess but also in Chand's hut. There were also parrots, rock pigeons, pheasants, *mainas*, a bear, barking deer, rabbits and a monkey. Chand made special efforts when he explained an orchid that looked familiar to a male or female organ.

He was once photographed by Kanwal while explaining an orchid to a stunning beauty from a tea estate, who was standing rather close. Major Cooper showed to Chand and appreciated it, suggesting it must be shown to Mrs. Chand Ram. Chand missed a heart beat or two. There were free drinks in the evening. God was merciful; Cooper soon got posted to some other Unit before the joke could be prolonged for some more treats.

THUNDER AND TRANQUILITY

The very mention of Sela-Bomdila-Rupa-Tenga conjured up enough elation since it had not been exploited much till 1964 and had managed to keep its originality. The aborigines thrived. The drive on serpentine roads, along the rivers and rivulets was thrilling. The frequent landslides added to the spice.

The treachery of China was ever hurting. The General commanding the force there was a terror – a need of times. A thorough professional, no-nonsense person, ethical to the core, he minced no words. He had a real manly personality, a big turban on a large face, red shot eyes and a well poised soldierly frame. He had a resonant commanding voice, which all respected and feared equally. Irresolute, timid, unprofessional, physically weak, pot-bellied or lacking in conduct always got a mouthful and downsizing. Those who could look straight into his searching, piercing eyes and talk straight from their heart won his admiration. Anant was of the last kind.

Anant's Unit was part of the Brigade which was loaned to the Division, responsible for the defence of this region. Though attachment was an operational necessity, the Brigade was an eye sore for being an outright winner in all professional and sports competitions. The last competition was inter-battalion firing. Anant's Battalion was way ahead; the second managed only 52 precent of the points scored by the former.

The General got all the Brigade and Battalion Commanders together, asking all other officers to vacate the Red Ball Institute. Among the juniors, only Duggal and Kanwal were witness to the spectacle since they were responsible for the conduct of the prize distribution ceremony and lunch. The General made all Commanding Officers stand at attention, except Anant, who was at ease along with the Brigade Commanders. He then blew his top and got real nasty when he said "All of you buggers should be attached to Anant's Battalion for training."

There was a lull for a while. Anant displayed modesty through a very tight mouth, stiff eyes and wrinkles on forehead. There was disappointment, remorse, unhappiness on the faces of all others who had faced the General's wrath. How long?

Soon permission was granted by the General and beer and gin started flowing. There was amazing din of discussions, laughter and healthy downsizing of each other, when one of the officers confronted the General and said, “Sir, we have requested Anant to arrange for lodging and boarding while we are attached for training.” The General looked at the officer, slowly parting his lips to a grin and remarked, “You buggers will never change,” followed by a big swig of beer and a thundering laughter.

COMMANDERS ON LOOK OUT

The General and Commanders, except Anant’s boss, were out to Tezpur for a seminar. *Baisakhi* was being celebrated in the *Gurudwara*, which all Officiating Commanders and Officiating Division Commander attended. Thereafter, they all moved to the Mess. The ‘session’ started without any waste of time. All Commanders were sitting in a group.

A newly commissioned officer, a namesake of the General, was called upon and briefed. Then they took a dig at his namesake, “You bugger, you have no manners. What have you learnt so far, you bugger? You bully your subordinates. Stop it, otherwise you will be chastised.” They continued, “Where have you vanished with your Commanders? For training at higher Headquarters? We declare you deserters and hereby take over the command of higher echelons.” The joke continued for the day, much to the rejoicing of all.

Following the seminar, the General held a conference to convey the decisions taken by the higher-ups. “Good Morning, Gentlemen. I am happy to be back amongst you all after a week and I have a sigh of relief that all remained well in the Formation. You all have shown flair for higher ranks. From the on goings that I have heard I am proud to say that all of you are fit to take on higher responsibilities. Of course, you all buggers will have to live it with us while we are here.”

The young namesake of the General told his colleagues, “I vow to emulate my senior commanders to become an exasperating ‘bugger’ General.”

WIN-WIN SITUATION

The village of Rupa comprising about 200 huts was to the South of Rupa River flowing into Bhutan. The loaned Brigade was given responsibility to defend the Western approach from Bhutan taking defences on both sides of the river and road along it. The highest ground Dabang Phu was with Anant's Battalion. To ascertain the standard of defences of the Brigade, an exercise was planned. The exercise started with an imaginary enemy based on Chinese organization and their strategy and tactics. A senior Major from artillery was deputed to be the Umpire and also to depict situations as enemy moved to attack, and the defenders responded by physical movement; the Umpire noting reflexes and giving decisions.

The battle started. Fifteen days of movement of the enemy was synchronized in 30 minutes. Their bombardment, aggressive patrolling and mini skirmishes were depicted. Probing attacks to know about the Dabang Phu forces and their defense preparations were launched by the enemy. The situations were being painted as realistically as possible. The attack by the imaginary enemy ensued. Anant had deputed Harbans,–Second-in-Command to look after the Umpire, Shashi.

Harbans meanwhile had managed to escort Shashi to the Mess bunker since it had become uncomfortable for the Umpire to sit outside in the wintry cold at a height of about 9,000 feet. Shashi being crucial to report on the Battalion's performance was the guest of honour. Harbans's offer of first shot of whisky did help delaying the declaration of casualties. But two drinks more and the battle became brisk. The Umpire got the required inspiration to become virtually the Commander of the imaginary enemy to decimate the so called impregnable defenses of Dabang Phu. He started painting rather impractical and non-pragmatic situations, and at such a speed that time was inadequate to respond methodically.

Understanding the gravity of the situation, Harbans instructed, "Kalu Ram, the enemy is very close. Remove the patromax and the glasses. We are being seen by the enemy. Now drinks and snacks later." Kalu Ram rose to the occasion.

Harbans moved out to respond to the picture painting. After a little while Shashi followed out. In that extreme cold, against the resolute fight of the Dabang Phu defenders, enemy attacks started failing. Well before midnight the enemy attack petered out. The Unit had well attended to its casualties, damaged weapons had been correctly disposed off to the rear, citations for the brave had been accounted for, and the "Chinese prisoners" had been interviewed and escorted to higher Headquarters.

Kalu Ram was in full action. Harbans had been recommended for award. The Umpire was satisfied with his knowledge and skill.

A win-win situation indeed.

THREE-IN-ONE

After the Indo-China War of 1962, there were feverish efforts to improve in all the fields. New weapons and equipment were being procured from abroad and being assimilated. Strategy and tactics were being honed. However, in the North-East Frontier Agency (NEFA), the necessity to have defences along the line of high hills at Nathu La, or even much in the rear at Sela were yet not possible due to an acute shortage of resources and also in the background of a jolt received owing to the superiority of Chinese forces and the deception, speed and efficiency of their attacks.

The defences thus were consolidated at the heights surrounding Bomdi La. Undoubtedly, the defenses here were impregnable.

The Division of four Infantry Brigades had three Battalions on its order of battle of the same group, the Sikh Regiment, one each in three different Brigades. To try out the strength of the defence system, the Brigade deployed at Rupa area was given the task of acting as actual enemy. Since the attacker per se required much bigger force, the "enemy Brigade's" strength shown on ground was to be considered four times. The enemy Brigade also had a Sikh Battalion. The "enemy" occupied area around Dirang Dzong, a beautiful open patch with a shimmering river. The area was midway between Sela and Bomdi La. The "enemy forces" advanced, employing Chinese army tactics and occupied hills opposing Bomdi La, poised for attack.

Two days prior to the envisaged attack, patrolling by both the sides was in full swing; by the enemy to probe the defences and to select the best direction of attack, and by the defender to dominate the area in front and also to find out enemy's direction and probable day of main attack. Suddenly, "enemy Battalion" noticed some confusion and kind of heated argument going on among all *Sikh* troops about 700 feet below their position. As it transpired, these were two patrols, one each from the Battalions of different Brigades of Bomdi La defences. They both were claiming victory over the other for one laying an ambush and the other of its success in breaking through. They both were convinced that the other party was the "enemy troops". The junior rank umpires with them were also confused as to who was friend or foe.

The "enemy Battalion" quickly mustered about 12 men, depicting 50, who moved stealthily down the slopes through the jungle area, surrounded the arguing troops and took them as prisoners of war. The whole task had been accomplished meticulously and the umpires declared so. As to who were the Indian troops and who were the "Chinese" it became clear by looking at the stripes of some men of the "enemy" group which were golden yellow in colour against white ones worn by the arguing groups. In the *Sikh* regiment, only one Unit, 4 *Sikh* had the tradition of wearing yellow stripes. Also now the two arguing parties, 16 and 17 *Sikh* realized that enemy troops were not wearing camouflage nets on their headgears as against they themselves, a distinguishing feature in the exercise to differentiate between a friend and foe.

Notwithstanding the ill-fated "capture" of some troops of Bomdi la forces, the "enemy" could not make much headway against the impregnable defence system.

HUSH HUSH HASH

Guri was Inder's best pal. Guri belonged to a landlord family from Haridwar, while Inder was the son of a politician-businessman family of Delhi. The families of the two also had properties at Saharanpur. They stayed for days and days together. Kanwal was close to Inder, being a relative and childhood friend. Kanwal had the family trait of a hunter, and at that a good one.

Guri offered a hunting trip to the jungles in Haridwar, with due permission from the authorities. Dhanni, also a relative, living in the same colony as that of Inder, who had no idea of a gun or hunting, also chipped in. All were in their 20s, Inder being the eldest and Kanwal the youngest.

Three of them from Delhi, with two guns, plenty of ammunition of all the numbers for small and big game, started in Inder's Ambassador, stayed the night with a friend at Dehradun, reaching Haridwar by about 10 in the morning next day. In the April of 1966, the weather had started getting warmer and they all were thirsty, particularly because of the liquor consumed the previous night.

Guri received them with open arms and offered plenty of homemade buttermilk and '*mathis*'. They decided to pay homage at the Har Ka Pauri, the most sacred place along the Holy Ganges. Guns and ammunition, including Guri's, were secured in a cupboard in the hotel room.

On the entrance to the Pauri there was a shop where '*shardai*', a sweetened mixture of water, milk, sugar, meshed almonds and musk melon seeds–a real tasty and relishing cold drink for summers–was available. The shopkeeper had his hair tied in a neat knot, had a flowing grayish beard, fair complexion and a big orange coloured *'tikka'* on his forehead.

While making *'shardai* he gave a mischievous smile, a slight wink, and asked if he should add a bit of special sweetener. The *'shikaris'* looked at each other in doubt. The handsome shopkeeper insisted, "A little *'bhang'* (marijuana) to kill the heat". And he took the decision himself, added the substance and handed over the glasses.

The *'shardai'* was sweet, chilled, nourishing and just too delicious. Satisfied, they went round the sacred place and also on the large cemented area in the middle of the river. There, while picking up water from the river, Inder went a few steps down, and that is where he saw in the opposite enclosed area several female legs uncovered up to the knee. All four of them washed their eyes as if real devotees again and again. They felt thirsty.

It did not take much time to the *'shardai'* shop, where they gulped two to three glasses each, complaining to the shopkeeper that his sweetener was no good. He advised them to eat some sweets. In the bazaar, the first thing they saw was a woman in half *'ghungat'* carrying a round flat utensil full of *'rabri'*, the thickened sweet milk. It had cardamom seeds and a white shining *'vark'* (foil) on it. All four had three to four plates each.

The effect started playing. Their minds began swirling and drifting. Titillation to eat more engulfed their thoughts. Bananas vanished from a vendor, followed by some *'barfi'* washed down with water from a municipal tap. Kanwal sat down to smoothen the sensation, expecting others to follow suit. But Inder, putting his arms out, started imitating an aircraft; Guri and Dhanni, put their arms around each other and walked about talking irrelevantly. Ultimately, they did reach their hotel room by three in the afternoon. The hunting time was fixed at four. Thankfully, Guri had forgotten the cupboard keys in the jeep down below. In any case, guns and hunting were not on their minds, their thoughts were uncontrollable.

Dhanni suddenly started laughing, continuing thereafter louder and louder, and his hand clutching his stomach. Inder's outstretched arms had started moving up and down, keeping up with a lurching body; tongue out with a gurgling sound — very much a bear that he was simulating. Guri lied down on the bed with one leg and one hand in the air for a few minutes and then changing to the other pair, doing a self created yoga exercise. Each time he changed his posture he gave a hullaballoo like a barking deer, sobbing all the time interspersed with word 'mama.' Kanwal, a soldier, was trying to put his thoughts together, but failed miserably. His head was swirling faster than the wheels of an aircraft about to take off. A severe, piercing headache took over.

Dhanni's cheekbones had started aching because of constant laughing and crying. Inder was looking stupefied through continuous exercise, now his pelvis moving forward and backward; Guri started sobbing; Kanwal with a splitting headache, sitting next to him, was singing a lullaby in his most monotonous tone, neither he nor Guri knew what he was singing. Guri could not be calmed.

When did they go to sleep, how many times each got up to drink water from a large size pitcher or went to the bathroom was not known.

In the morning, Guri's two men came and woke up the foursome and narrated their story that they had waited throughout the night at the designated place with large mosquitoes devouring them. They had seen two herds of '*barasingha*', a pair of blackbucks, heard barking deers and grunting of wild boar. All four hunters heard the report, regretting what they had missed. Their eyes were red, they felt hungry, lethargic and minds clouded with loss, shame and sorrow. All thanked their stars for being fortunate to be at least alive to pledge another excursion but without alluring '*shardai*'.

4

Trundling Along

WINING IN OF A YOUNG OFFICER IN '*SARDAR* MESS'

They were located at Poonch at the highest hills in that area of Pir Panjal Ranges A smart young officer, Second Lieutenant H.S. Panag (Babbu) with a military background was posted to the Unit on being commissioned from the Indian Military Academy, Dehradun. As was the tradition in the Unit, a young officer was always looked after as the 'babe' of the Unit and groomed in the best possible manner. Besides being taken around the Unit and introduced to maximum possible personnel, he was wined in the Junior Commissioned Officers' (JCOs) Mess, also known as '*Sardar* Mess', and dined in Officers' Mess. As customary, he was accompanied by a mature senior officer to make him feel at ease, behave, drink mildly and learn the proprieties of the immediate subordinates.

Enroute, walking to the *Sardar* Mess, which was just half a kilometer away, Kanwal advised Babbu how to conduct himself, talk less, listen more and not to get drunk. He told the youngster that *Sardars* were known for their hospitality which they wished must end into officers getting 'glad', a more respectable term referring to someone completely smashed. Kanwal also cautioned, "Babbu, ensure the drink is poured into your glass and not that your glass is taken and poured into another glass jostling with a neat

Patiala. Have small sips so as there is less scope for any additions." And then sternly, he inquired, "Are you listening?"

The youngster replied, "Yes sir."

Kanwal added further, "Ensure that I am not let down and you don't make a fool of yourself and a sick man tomorrow."

The youngster assured, "Right sir, I will follow your instructions."

Kanwal, who was the Adjutant, said "You better as well do."

The *Sardars* were in great cheer, looking forward to Sunday, the next day being off. They did play all their tricks on the youngster who steadfastly dealt with their tactics admiringly, in good senses till the end, except gobbling up all the tasty snacks offered.

Sardars concentrated upon Kanwal in the name of the great Battalion and his established prowess to drink a good quantity. He forgot his own advice given to the youngster and accepted some stuff from each of the glass brought to him by the waiter and offered by a *Sardar*. Two or three times he allowed his left over, dropped into the neat Patiala pegs. His self designated one hour was added by another half an hour.

The officers thanked the *Sardars* and moved back to their Mess. A few meters and Kanwal started wavering, thoroughly sozzled, hitting into the hill sometimes, balancing, and again hugging the rock. The youngster came to his rescue, holding him tight to ensure he did not fall on the steep side of the hill.

Kanwal floundering, said, "You, you behaved well. I am happy. Always be like this. Now come on and take me to my room and not to the Mess." The youngster literally dragged and carried him to the room.

Kanwal, appreciating, said, "Good. Now Babbu, tell all in the Mess that I am not feeling well. Behave there. No more drink for you now, and thanks."

Kanwal entered his room, cement in his head, stomach doing somersault and feet wobbling. While taking off his turban, a look in the mirror showed him bleary eyed. Something coaxed him 'quick'. He jumped to the bathroom, spewed out horrendous stuff with loud roaring and gurgling sounds. Perhaps became the young officer himself.

TWEEDLEDUM AND TWEEDLEDEE

The beautiful valley of Sonamarg, 'Meadows of Gold' was surrounded by high rocky hills, snow-clad sinewy mountains and gorges that defied gravity. The road to it had rolling hills of green meadows on either side and there were tall trees that made the area unbelievably picturesque. The River Sindh carved the valley.

The location of a military training school had all the advantages to teach the students rock climbing, crossing of fast rivulets, jungle lore at a height above 9000 feet, movement on snow, survival and living on glacier. John Dias, Narender Kumar and H S Ahluwalia, the famous conquerors of Mount Everest were the instructors. The school was a little ahead of the mini township, just a few feet higher than nine thousand feet to qualify for high altitude rations, which comprised apart from usual- almonds, big and small raisins, condensed milk, fruits besides enhanced meats, chicken, sardines, luncheon meat, ham and a tote of daily rum.

The religion-based Regiments of Indian Army constitute two very interesting ones, drawing men mainly from Punjab — these are SIKH and SIKH LI. All Sikhs except the scheduled castes comprise the Sikh Regiment, while the latter are in the Sikh LI. Men of the Sikh Regiment, being from traditionally upper castes had the advantage at that time of a better lookout, élan and attitude. The men of Sikh LI thus were always at loggerheads with them to compete, causing perpetual rivalry and friction between them.

Gurdial Singh of the Sikh Regiment was Kanwal's helper while Gujjar Singh of LI was with Tirath. The irony was that Gurdial was dark in complexion, had a scanty beard and not a very flattering physique. On the other hand, Gujjar was handsome, with a rolled beard, tied a good turban and possessed a majestic demeanor that caused even more bitterness as Gurdial could not swallow his better personality. Even Tirath's experience of ex-Sikh Regiment as a soldier and now in Sikh LI as an officer could not put the horse in front of the cart.

Hence, almost daily there were diatribes that had to be sorted out as there was no dearth of confrontations between the two diehards, Gujjar and Gurdial, especially since Tirath and Kanwal shared the same tent being batch mates and good friends. The tricks were shabby. Kanwal found his dry rations in his shoes, Gurdial blamed Gujjar. One bottle of Tirath's ration rum was found half emptied in Gurdial's locked box, as Gujjar smiled gleefully.

However, both Gujjar and Gurdial had great admiration for their '*sahibs*' who were buddies during the course. Once while doing rock climbing on a nasty hillside, Kanwal had rappelled down to a lower rock, while he was being supported by a rope held by Tirath from top. He was waiting for Tirath to follow when out of carelessness Kanwal slipped. Tirath lost his hold on the rock but was mercifully saved from falling, though suffered an injury. He in his report told the authorities that the mistake was his own and no one else was to be blamed.

On another occasion while crossing a river, Tirath got washed away by the fast current to a rock, and Kanwal, a good swimmer, took to himself to rescue his friend. Kanwal was held with a rope by another officer as he swam in ice-cold water till the mid stream from where he threw a rope towards Tirath. After several efforts Tirath caught the rope. Tirath and Kanwal were slowly pulled back to the bank to the applause of all. They were numb to the limb. A magnanimous instructor offered them shots of neat brandy. The instructors were satisfied that their students had successfully come out of a difficult situation and that their training had instilled the spirit of courage, resoluteness and comradeship in them.

These stories spread like wild fire. After learning how their *'sahibs'* were making sacrifices for each other, Gujjar and Gurdial were transformed.

They were found sleeping together with their arms on each other's shoulders with an empty bottle of rum next to them, with some plastic jars safely kept on the shelf, containing all types of dry fruits that were the ration of officers.

LOVE STRICKEN; BOUNTIES OF NATURE!

Close to the training camp of Sonamarg, there was one of the most majestic and beautiful glaciers. The Thajiwas, 'The Valley of Glaciers', was about seven kilometers from Sonamarg, and upwards many kilometers in depth. Kanwal and five other youngsters decided a picnic on a Sunday. Equipped with *'tandoori'* chicken, *'rogan josh', 'paranthas'*, pickles and beer bottles, they walked up to one of the most beautiful spots upstream.

In the background were snow-clad mountains, slightly lower were snow patches around rhododendron bushes, further lower some green patches of emerald green grass and then dozens of small streams through the shoals; mingling, splitting, producing music, joining again to become bigger, faster, rippling over stones, curving rocks, gushing downwards, rushing into a full fledged stream. These were picture-postcard views. There was no breeze and the sun was exuding warmth in an otherwise extremely cold place.

The place was a great attraction for the tourists. The youngsters were applauded by dozens of civilians about three kilometers downstream, meandering their way spread into a long half a kilometer queue. They carried handbags, thermoses and cameras, slowly crawling their way. They cluttered about in several groups. After throwing hurried looks at the older folks, gents and children, the young officers turned towards the "*attractions*", which looked rather pretty in their pants, Punjabi suits, jackets and some wearing caps and mufflers.

More people drifted in, the spread becoming larger, necessitating crossing of water channels to dry spots. A God sent opportunity for the youngsters. Kanwal along with other friends soon volunteered and started helping them to cross the channels, their boots submerged in cold water but totally unmindful of it, the scintillation of soft touch was enough to keep them warm. The holding of hands, shoulder supporting and almost lifting them up continued for about an hour or so. But Alas! Weather seemed to be packing up.

People hurried to their food, ready to assemble their nick-knack and move back. Help was again forthcoming. The '*kafila*' of beauty, fragrance and mirth sauntered its way downwards.

The youngsters guzzled some more chilled beer, shoved cold chicken and '*paranthas*' through lampooned throats, with yet no desire to move back. The Thajivas severe cold winds, fast descending clouds and a heavy downpour had no mercy on their melancholy hearts. Only the military discipline and order of the day came to their rescue in the form of raincoats that they carried.

Thereafter, the remaining days of training were a drag with everyone longing to get down to Srinagar and then proceed to their hometowns for some leave.

SMALL PEGS : '*CHOTTAS*'

ONE

Major Harbhajan, the Officiating Commanding Officer was going about, with Kanwal tugging along, when a jawan came by and saluted Harbhajan.

Harbhajan: "Yes Kaka, You had gone on leave, how is everybody at home?"

Joginder: "Sir, with your blessings everything is fine."

Harbhajan: "OK then, go and do your job nicely."

Joginder: "Sir, happy news, I got a son."

Harbhajan: "I am happy to know that, congratulations and '*shabash*'."

Joginder: "It is all with your kindness."

Harbhajan: "In this, Joginder, what is my kindness got to do with it."

TWO

The news was that the new Commanding Officer will soon be in, which ushered in happiness among all since the new combatant was from their outfit only, known for his sterling leadership qualities. Harbhajan, a friend of Ajit, took upon himself to prepare the Unit to its best to duly welcome the latter. There was so much of enthusiasm that Harbhajan who had never worn the full equipment, including the big pack on the back, starting wearing it. Nobody was allowed to touch his pack except his batman for reasons unknown.

But during a lunch break in a long march, the Commanding Officer wanted to lie down for a while and unknowingly picked up Harbhajan's pack to be used as a pillow and found it to be rather light. Well, it had to be since it carried only an air filled pillow, fulfilling the requirement of the time.

THREE

Pargan was a rogue of the highest order. About five feet and eight inches tall, dark complexioned, thick snobbish features and a hefty frame, he was an outstanding wrestler. His hands and feet were rather large, true to the adage, 'large head and brain of the intelligentsia and large feet and hands of the stupid.'

Another trait, he once sodomised a young soldier and threatened him with dire circumstances if he reported it to anyone. When Pargan tried again, the boy ran away and complained. Before the authorities could lay hands upon Pargan, he got hold of the boy and while trying to strangulate him, broke his arm instead. Pargan was taken to charge and was dismissed from service and given seven years of rigorous imprisonment in a civil jail. Since considered dangerous, he was kept in a separate tent, duly manacled, and awaiting the arrival of civil police to take him into their custody.

Pargan had picked up the hair of horse's tail from the area while going for nature's call and tied three rings of the manacles which used to be opened for that duration. As usual, keeping the prescribed length of the manacle between the two ankles, it was locked by the guard.

At about midnight, Pargan broke the hair, took one hand out of the handcuff, a miracle indeed, crawled from under the tent into the jungle and walked throughout the night, reached some village where he got his manacle and handcuff broken on some deal, which perhaps he never fulfilled befooling the blacksmith. The vagabond got some yellow cloth from somewhere, applied ash on his forehead and posing as a '*sadhu*' moved into deeper jungles.

For three days, numerous parties of five personnel each had searched for him at railway stations, bus stands of towns in the area, villages and jungles. One party got the clue from a village about the '*sadhu*', chased him and found him about 18 miles away from the Unit in a field engaged in a sadistic act with a country boy. When found surrounded, he said, "Just a minute, please."

He got the butt of the rifle on his right cheek, blood gushed out, he toppled over, and was overpowered. In the scuffle he got his left hand thumb also fractured. But back in the Unit, he did demonstrate how he had softened his hand by massage and slided it out of the cuffs.

Instead of waiting for the police from Punjab, he was taken there with a strong posse of army personnel.

FOUR

A young officer's training in a Unit would start at lower levels so as the leader and the led understood each other. In a Sepoy to Lance Naik cadre, Kanwal being the senior most always sat on the right of a squad of 10 men, as was the custom. The instructor was the legendary Naik Joginder, who being mischievous as he was, would always make the officer demonstrate all examples by saying, "Now to demonstrate, number one from the right to get up and fall-in behind the weapon." Thus, there was always extra fatigue for Kanwal.

Kanwal decided to sit on the left of the class, expecting Joginder as usual, to call number one from the right to demonstrate. Joginder saluted him seeking permission to start. And then, "Now, we will demonstrate how a machine gun is carried up slung on shoulder for hundred yards. To give example, fall-in number one from the left."

FIVE

To revive sports, a number of Inter-Company tournaments were held. Second Lieutenant Balraj Bakshi was told to conduct volleyball tournament. At his hometown, 'v' and w" used to be pronounced as 'b'. True to the learnt legacy, on the board it was written, "Inter-Company Bolleyball Tournament."

SIX

Football finals were between a Sikh and a Kumaon Battalion, being played in the Kumaon Unit. The spectators were in hundreds, including personnel of other Units and locals. Match started smoothly, both sides showing their best skills. However, soon it started turning ugly, with both sides resorting to foul play. Both the teams had arguments with the referee. Soon there was fist play between the teams and situation went out of control.

Kumaoni spectators started pelting stones, and Sikhs not to be left behind took out the long bamboos from the tents and for a few minutes it was free for all. In order to diffuse the situation, Kumaoni Officer Major Sapru took out his revolver, fired in the air and shouted, "Stop." The fighting did stop. Men moved back to their sides. The match was postponed. Sapru's revolver was lost.

The Commanding Officers were called to the higher Headquarters the next day and given a mouthful. Match was ordered to be replayed the next day. It was then that the Commander asked the Commanding Officer of the Sikh Battalion to return the Kumaoni revolver. The Commanding Officer was not aware of this development.

As he entered his Unit, he saw Regimental Police Havildar Mehanga Singh coming from the opposite direction. Soon Mehanga's past flashed across his mind. He called him. Mehanga took no time in taking out the revolver from his pocket, with an empty case that was fired in the air on the day of the match, and five live rounds.

SEVEN

Mehanga Singh's achievements were well known. He did everything with great aplomb. His dominating structure, with an ever shining naughty eyes, beard tied upwards with a thick thread, long moustache, a patterned turban, a smart turn out, had a fertile mind where something was always cooking.

Sometime in 1960, when the Unit was in Ambala, in erstwhile Punjab, it was given barracks close to the railway station. Numerous guests from the villages used to visit, thus wheat was always falling short. To their good luck, a train full of wheat bags was parked close by. At night, Mehnga and some others broke the seal of one of the wagons and emptied its contents in their cook houses. Thereafter, holes were made into a couple of sacks and these were taken to an adjoining Unit, falling wheat making a tell tale sign. The court of inquiry blamed the innocent Unit.

However, the Commander could not reconcile. He held direct discussion with the Commanding Officer of the tricky Unit and learnt the truth. Railways could find nothing.

Mehanga was promoted to Lance Naik and was assigned to Regimental Police Section, since only a rogue could stop other rogues from wrong doings, knowing the tricks of the trade.

EIGHT

The Unit was a distance away from the supply point and there were restrictions on the use of military transport. The bringing of fresh rations and meat was a perpetual problem. What to do?

The innovative, improvising and mischievous mind of Mehanga started ticking. He soon found a rickshaw yard; wherefrom the rickshaw pullers used to get the rickshaws taken on rent to ply throughout the day, to eke out a living. He got two other chivalrous ones recruited for his scheme. They all went there on one cycle, picked up two rickshaws, peddled to the bushy area, ripped open the seats and covers, buried them into the sand, demolished any signs of the mischief and came to the Unit just before day break. The good carpenter was awakened. He already had some railway sleepers hidden, a brainchild and enterprise of Mehanga. He cut them to size and fixed them where just yesterday were the beautiful seats and canopies.

There never was a problem of supplies getting stale or delayed. Mehanga had got qualified for promotion to Naik.

NINE

The Unit was due for inspection, immediately after moving to Ferozepur, in Punjab. The lines allotted were shabby and there were no green plants. The Commanding Officer was distressed. He was to leave for some emergency for a few days and was to return just a day before the inspection. He expressed his dismay to all, especially to the Subedar Major, while Mehanga was within earshot.

The Commanding Officer returned on completion of his duty and as he entered the Unit on Saturday, he found hundreds of healthy plants of all kinds welcoming him. Surprised, he was quite annoyed on being fooled about fake flower branches. He was told it was not so. He got down from the jeep and tried to pull a plant but couldn't. Monday's went off extremely well, the Inspection Officer specially mentioning the greenery and the aesthetic sense of the Unit. The Commanding Officer was pleased.

On Wednesday, there was a letter from the company garden, a civilian concern that about 300 flower plants had been stolen along with flowerpots. The Commanding Officer smiled on how the evidence of flowerpots had been buried.

TEN

The New Year Eve at Digboi club in Assam was a treat, particularly their selection of Miss Digboi. The bachelors, and also the forced ones, looked around with roving eyes, throbbing hearts, and wicked smiles. What a beautiful creation of female form she was, just having ushered in her 17th year, wide black eyes, high cheekbones, full lips, smooth chin on a long fair neck on slightly naked rounded shoulders and such stunning curves. She walked majestically — all eyes riveted in admiration of rhythmic buttocks.

Bakshi couldn't resist the temptation to dance with the miracle, though his knowledge of dancing was limited to '*kabaddi*'. He literally swept the girl off her feet and swirled about the dancing floor. Two or three tapped on his shoulders to change partners, which he construed as encouragement for his excellence in dancing style.

Fortunately, at midnight the lights went off for a few seconds, followed by full lights with a resounding applause of 'Happy New Year'. Bakshi had smeared the girl's lips with his hot love through his twirled up moustache. Somehow the partners of the most "spectacular dance of the evening" were separated with Miss Digboi making a hasty retreat to freshen up as prize distribution had been announced.

Harbhajan had seen Bakshi dancing, searched for him, pushed his thick moustache up showing a bit of lips as much as he could and said, "Look after us oldies also."

The prizes were given for various events, the last three being to the three beauties. And the very last prize of course went to the "Dancer of the Gone Year."

INNATE DIEHARD

'Raja' was a misnomer. He was actually a raja by trade, a barber. Way back in 1917, when he was a small boy, he was left in the Unit. He remembered the *'firangi'* as much as he liked their steadfastness, resoluteness and justice. But he disliked their disdainful snooty attitude and latent animosity towards the Indians.

He was in the Unit without any recruitment. He provided his services only to Indians. He was not allowed to cut hair, shave or trim nails of the British, perhaps because of his crude instruments that he had learnt to use — a set of three scissors of differing sizes and shapes, shaving blade which he used without the handle and a file with one side sharpened like a knife and the other crushed to shape like a shovel head. He had a stone to sharpen his instruments along with a black leather bag made by the Unit cobbler to carry all his paraphernalia.

The Unit of about 900 men had Sikhs and Muslims as soldiers while all others were a happy mix of many communities, be it cooks, cobblers, sweepers, carpenters, blacksmiths, mechanics, armourers or water carriers who also duplicated as buglers.

Was he a Sikh? Was Harnam Singh his actual name? When had he started tying a spotlessly clean turban, nobody knew. Nor was there any knowledge on how he rolled his beard, how he secured permission to wear white *'kurta-pyjama'* and eat in any of the six cook houses. His complexion was jet black, beard and moustache white. He spoke with a roundness of his blackish lips puffing out a little air, which at times produced a whistle like sound.

Very few remembered that in 1946, he had told every Indian that when he had gone to the *'firangi'* quarters (that of British), to meet the guards there, he had been told that *'gora memsahibs'* were packing and thus India will be independent very soon. He warned all not to tell anyone else since the information was only for the individual he was talking to in full confidence. He knew how Muslims had departed from the Unit.

He was a story teller, innocent informer, adviser, guide and soothsayer. All this he did for the sole purpose; the aggrandizement of the Unit. He was an institution in himself.

His failing sight could not be salvaged by his generally dirty thick glasses, and thus many times he cut nails too deep to cause pain, persisting for a day or two, left a waft of hair on the jaw or cut an uneven moustache. All was pardoned in the harangue of the tranquilizing experiences of the *'angrez'* who was a baddie and his client who was a hero.

Did he die in the Unit itself or after leaving it? When did he leave the Unit? Who knew of his last days with the Unit? Since he was an institution, did he leave any legacy? Did he ever marry? If so, what became of that? Only a few who knew about him were alive now. Only gibble gabble in the passing might be said about him when the oldies met.

In his day, he had carried a self imposed discipline upon himself to support the unique system of the elements that make a Unit an entity. Raja had vanished as hugger-mugger as he had come to the Unit. Some institutions survive only during their lifetimes.

WHY KANWAL?

Cooper was worldly wise, relaxed, and carefree and won't go out of the way to do anything practical though he liked to be appreciated for his desk job. Darshan was placed under him as the senior JCO (Junior Commissioned Officer). Darshan, earlier a signaler, was handsome and articulate. An excellent basketball player and an athlete in his time, he was assigned to 'D' (Delta) Company.

The outfit had become notorious for ill discipline. Some men had inculcated the habit of tobacco chewing and smoking which was the result of loose handling by the chain smoker Company Commander. The Company had maximum overstay leave, absent without leave and stealth cases besides trimming of beard and infighting.

Darshan was more of a sportsman than a professional leader or administrator. Therefore, the state of affairs in the Company further worsened. Orders were received to move the Unit to a peace station after tenure of almost three and half years in the tough field. Cooper had also meanwhile moved out of the Unit on staff.

It was expected that some experienced officer would be posted to Delta to improve its fortunes. Sudden orders and Kanwal with less than three years of service was assigned the Company. For some reason, the CO was annoyed with Kanwal two days back, and so Kanwal took his new appointment as a kind of punishment.

Next day, in the office, Kanwal to Duggal, who was the Adjutant: "Sir, I want to speak to the CO regarding my posting to the worst Company to Command".

Duggal: "Futile attempt. You know the CO. You will rather 'buy' it for questioning his decision."

Kanwal insisted. The CO reflected his now known natural-scornful-frown on his wheatish forehead, out of a tightly tied turban, darker than allowed, and in his reserved but piercing tone asked, "Yes?"

Kanwal: "Sir, I must have done something wrong that I am being punished and posted to the worst Company?"

CO: "So, what do you want?"

Kanwal: "Sir, I beg for your kind reconsideration. A more mature and experienced officer can improve this Company while I can learn to command in an established Company."

CO, with his cut-to-pieces manner, "Who are you to decide worst Company? Are you telling me my job, where to send you? Will you go to Delta and do your duty? I had been Company Commander of this Company myself for several years before Cooper had taken over. Now carry on."

Kanwal felt disgusted, agitated and helpless. His having done excellently in instruction courses, professional duties and sports seemed to be coming to '*naught*'. Why was he in the army? Why in this Unit? Why under such an unsympathetic CO? Why was he serving in this lousy mountainous place, barren and hot? Suddenly black and grey clouds began building up.

In the evening, he played a basketball match between officers' and *JCO's* team in a foul temper, injured a couple of opponents, did not give pass to his CO properly, shouted at equals and was imprudent a couple of times towards his seniors.

Next day, he was summoned by the Adjutant to his office, who said, "Kanwal, what do you think you are? You were misbehaving and unsportsmanlike at the basketball match and sulking in the Mess. Your conduct has been noticed. You also seemed to have murmured to yourself when the CO was saying something. Fortunately for you he didn't notice it. I thought you were the bright one and would have taken a cue from what the CO had told you yesterday and the kind of confidence he has in your abilities. My advice as an elder brother - no more of any nonsense and do what you have been told to do, with the best of your abilities. I know my CO much more than you. He is going to support you to the hilt."

Kanwal persisted, "Sir, I still feel I will suffer there."

Duggal, cheesed off, "Enough of it! Get the hell out of here."

Kanwal was further depressed. He moved towards his Company with a heavy heart. He was welcomed by a beaming Darshan, met other JCOs and men while going round the Company. He tried the men's food and found it insipid. He went through Company files in an otherwise well maintained office. He had mixed feelings as to how the men would take it, after all they had been seeing him for the last three years as a Company Officer in another Company, Battalion Quarter Master and officiating Adjutant for a few months when Duggal was on a course and leave. He ordered a '*durbar*' (when a Commander addresses the men and listens to their points and solves their problems.)

Somehow, he was listless for the remaining part of the day. He was a little more responsive in the Mess, had a couple of drinks, meals, some reading and sound sleep. There was no physical training the next morning, Saturday being an administration day. In the '*durbar*', he addressed the men with candor and conviction. He said, "It is my proud privilege to have been selected to serve with the finest. After all this has been CO's own. You have been doing extremely well. I am confident with your cooperation; I would be able to do my job correctly."

He spoke at length as to what were his expectations from them and what they could expect from him. He started believing his words and that was the beginning of his fondness for the men he was going to be with for several years to come. He was happy having a cup of tea with the men, satisfied in the office for positive responses and some improvement in the men's food. He was particularly amused to see men who trimmed their beard, tying black cords and putting on beard nets.

In the mess he was his usual self, playful, jovial and humourous. The mood was upswing. It had drizzled and was cool. The beautiful dark grey and black clouds produced an aroma that further lifted the soaring spirits. The CO appeared to be a gorgeous, empathetic and fatherly figure.

In days to come, people had begun to notice a sea change in Kanwal's Company.

Kanwal always cherished a hope that his CO's frowns would lessen a bit. That never happened. Smiles and outright appreciation rather deepened the furrows. Command of soldiers was, after all, a serious business.

5

Blessing and Bane

MILITARY SPECIAL

They moved to Missamari railway station in Assam to embark for their truly deserved tenure at a peace station. The railway station and the surrounding area were being misused by the railway staff and passengers for defecation, bathing and cooking.

Over 500 military personnel did add to the problem of space though they were not responsible for filth because of their own foolproof arrangements.

They were at the mercy of innumerable mosquitoes of all sizes. The men could tackle the large ones but the small, fast, naughty ones were not manageable. What to say of the tiniest who came in swarms producing a whining sound and got into eyes, nostrils, mouth and shirts. It was always a wonder to watch hundreds of them moving all around together, retaining the formation within a yard or so producing a constant whirr. To get rid of this nuisance, a person had to move his arms and head violently, like a woman under the spell of a tantric or make a retreat to a safer place and then return under the attack of another swarm. It could be the same swarm still chasing the victim.

After several calls to important railway authorities, about half of the demanded bogies came in four days and the remaining in next three days. The bogies were the oldest in the railway kitty, dark red, filthy, half of the fans and lights missing. They all had placards stating 'MILITARY SPECIAL' hung on them straight, diagonal or lopsided.

The ingenuity of the Unit personnel was put to test as despite such reluctant railway staff they managed to improve and repair many systems. The much awaited 'power' was received with great cheer. The engine took more than four hours to fill its belly with coal and water. The train was ready at 11 am on the reserve siding for military specials.

All the military drills of special bugle calls to embark, disembark, time for physical training, drill and meals etc., which had been practised at New Mall, in a marked out football ground, had been rehearsed at the railway station. Indication of moving the train at sharp 11.45 am had been given. All were seated and happy leaving the far off East.

The train finally showed signs of life at 2 pm. The men gave out their *'jaikaras'*. The train moved rearwards for a kilometer and half, to leave the military siding and then lurched forward to the platform awaiting the signal to move. What a disgusting wait! Men had their lunch and evening tea there itself.

Mercifully, the final bugle call for all to entrain was sounded and the engine whistled huskily, puffing out thick black soot and smoke from top, and hot steam from its side flying off dirt from the ground. And behold! The military special was on the roll. The men this time held up their *'jaikaras'* till well past the signaling pole, precariously close to the passing train. The army of dogs fed for days on military rations, looked at the slithering giant, with expressions of disregard, contempt and disconnection. The men in the last compartments observed aspirants with their tails up chasing a bitch with a tail wrapped around her precious self, through the hind legs pressed against her underbelly.

August 1965 had its full share of rains, barely allowing any movement outside the train at the stoppages, since only water was all around. Stoppages were not only at the designated or mostly non-designated, almost abandoned railway stations, but also amidst two stations where some kind of duplicate track was available. These stoppages were essential to let some other passenger train pass. The train was also found missing to military authorities when to give a pass to a goods train, it was diverted to a sideline and thus whereabouts uncertain for eighteen hours. Thanks to immaculate planning whether fresh rations at selected stations were available or not, the Unit had ample supply of luncheon meat, tinned vegetables, eggs and dry rations. Of course, adequate liquor was also available.

Electricity in the train was a major problem. It was hot and humid. Generally the personnel were in shorts and vests, newspaper or a magazine furling about as fans and cussing as the stench emanating from the toilets due to train's long halts at stations was unbearable. The relief came only when the train moved and some breeze reached them; though full of smoke, soot or tiny coal pieces.

This was also the time when Indo-Pak relations had begun to deteriorate. There were straws in the wind of an imminent war. The surreptitious deployments by both the sides were taking place, defense systems studied and being improved.

The meter guage train had no emergency or urgency, so it took four days to reach Allahabad where there was stoppage for a day to switch to broad guage. The next train was quite in form, and it reached Ghaziabad in the morning at 10 am, to the sweet welcome music of silver band and spirited *'jaikaras'* by many at the railway station. Colonel Gurbaksh Singh, officers, JCOs and men from close by SIKH Regimental centre at Meerut Cantonment, serving and retired personnel from Delhi and adjoining areas had descended at the platform.

The stoppage of the train at that station had been extended by four hours. Drinks and eats, band tunes and guffaws had completely changed the face of the station into a hurly-burly place with abundant homogeneity, esprit-de-corps of a fraternity in frenzy. There was a repeat of the sorts at Delhi railway station, where an ex-CO, Colonel

Harwant Singh MC, then Commandant of a RAJRIF Regimental Center at Delhi Cantonment, with his band of hospitable people showered his affections and blessings.

The military special, ultimately, reached its destination Ferozepur, in six days against the normal schedule of three and half days. Immediate probability of a war made no difference to the accustomed systems of the time.

EXECUTION: PAR EXCELLENCE

(Sketches 4 and 5 enclosed)

Pakistan's much hallowed operations in 1947-48, of sending hordes of volunteers, civilians and soldiers, in the name of *'Jihad'* to capture the whole of Jammu and Kashmir (J&K), had failed miserably. The 'Instrument of Accession', signed by Maharaja Hari Singh of J&K had not found acceptance with its newly formed government. The great 'divide' and the largest exodus of people, a result of British mischief, individualistic political ambitions and shameful hit-in-the-back manoeuvers, had brought bad blood that bleeds the two nations even today.

The Indian forces' debacle of 1962 had emboldened the Pak forces, already getting aid of all kind except the troops, from the West, USA, some countries of Middle East and China, to venture an expedition against India in 1965.

All talks for peaceful settlement of issues had failed. Diplomacy had cracked. Armed forces, on both the sides, manoeuvered to defensive positions, eyeball to eyeball. Aggressive reconnaissance by air and ground had set in. Incursions across borders had started. Ultimately, on the pretext of India having opened the innings first at Cooch-Bihar, a fictitious paradox, Pakistan's air arm pounded Indian airfields. Pakistan launched Operation 'Grand Slam' across line of control to annex Jammu and Kashmir. India responded quickly, by opening up through international Border in Punjab.

4 *Sikh* (XXXVI), gloating in the glory of fighting a magnificent 25-day continuous battle at Walong in 1962,

was moved to a deserving peace station at Ferozepur, after a tenure of three and half years in the mountainous field of North-East. It had taken that much of time for Lieutenant Colonel Anant Singh's hard work and dedication to re-knit the team into an efficient fighting machine.

The Unit was amidst preparations for celebrations of Battle Honour Day Saragarhi on September 12 when the army got orders for mobilization. Zeroing of the newly received weapons was given top priority and all ranks were made to fire to get to know their weapons. There was no time to fire higher caliber weapons at the field firing ranges. Men were recalled from leave. The Battalion was placed at four hour notice on 3rd September to move to an undisclosed destination for an unspecified task.

Via Hari-Ke-Pattan, the famous bird sanctuary, it concentrated at Gilpan on 5th September, on its own side of the border, on road to Lahore. On 6th, it was first to cross the border and capture two Pak border outposts by two companies under Major Shamsher Singh Manhas and Major Dalip Singh Sidhu.

Kanwal, three years in service, with his Company had crossed the border at midnight and was awaiting further orders as a reserve to Shamsher's Company. The early morning was nippy; he wrapped himself in a water cape and closed his eyes lying on cold bare ground. As he just dozed off, he heard a sudden rattle of fire. He got up shivering with cold and fear. Soon enough, he got his nerves back and ordered his men to get ready to move.

Through the safe firm base provided by *Sikhs*, Indian 48 Infantry Brigade was launched for capture of Barki. 6/8 GR and 5 GUARDS, supported by CIH, cleared Hudiara Drain (4 kms) deep in enemy territory. Pak artillery was having a field day with advancing troops during the day. Enemy's Company by evening of 6th September at Hudiara drain was ultimately pushed back.

Men had learnt the necessity of digging a slit trench (about one and half to two feet deep) for protection for one or two persons, at the minutest lull in the movement. It provided safety unless a bomb landed directly on a person in the trench. And that is exactly what happened, when Kanwal sitting in a slit trench along with his helper, felt something hot and wet hitting his cheek and forearm. A direct hit on a soldier five yards away had his dozens of pieces flying about, leaving him badly mutilated and mud soaked half. Kanwal saw Shamsher, standing erect and giving instructions to a Junior Commissioned Officer. Kanwal suggested, "Sir, better to come in a trench." Shamsher smiled through his thick upright moustache and said, "The bullet meant for you shall always reach you." On night 7-8th September, the Battalion concentrated South-West of Village Brahmnabad.

On 8th September, 65 Infantry Brigade took over the advance. Village Brahmnabad was secured by Kanwal's Company in the morning, with some casualties, besides his mortar Junior Commissioned Officer laying down his life hit by a splinter from the enemy's airburst bomb. Village Barka Kalan was cleared by 9 *Madras*. 16 *Punjab* secured another village Barka Khurd right of the road. The enemy brought in intense and accurate artillery and mortar fire on the attackers. 4 *Sikh* suffered four killed and 19 wounded in this operation.

The enemy had made further move difficult with extremely strong positions at Barki along Icchogil canal to the rear, about 2,500 yards from the Indian troops. At 8 pm, orders were received to move north of the road in area Mile 16 after last light and be prepared by the morning of 9th September for any counterattack by the enemy.

Time was short, thus only slit trenches could be prepared. Hot meal had not been available since 5th evening. A meal, cooked a few kilometers to the rear, could be brought up either after sunset or before dawn, whenever there was some respite from the enemy's artillery fire and air attacks. At times, it did not reach the forward Companies.

Water was scarce. An old working hand pump in some village provided little water; otherwise the only source was standstill water in the paddy fields.

Destroyed mud houses, trampled drying fields and dead bodies of animals were seen everywhere. Weeping dogs were often heard at night, duly replied by howling jackals, silenced in fear by 'screech and thud' of artillery. No cremation for soldiers, except the burials with a stick or stone outside, the martyr's identity disc tied with it, for later recognition and respectful disposal.

9th September was a hot day and the Battalion had to remain in slit trenches without making any movement. Scorching heat enhanced acute thirst because of the paucity of water. Men showed remarkable water discipline.

On night 9-10th, patrols were sent out to obtain information about enemy defenses. Enemy was sensitive to any movement and responded by lighting up the area and a heavy barrage of fire. Lieutenant Colonel Anant Singh, had gone to the Brigade Tactical Headquarters, close to Hudiara. His words to the Unit on 5th September at Ferozepur, after *'ardas'* at Gurudawara Sahib, echoed in everyone's ears. These were:

> "An opportunity is likely to come by to achieve glory. In this war, God willing, we shall capture back the places from where we had been thrown out during the Partition. Remember the deeds of Saragarhi heroes and the gallant martyrs of 1962 operations; be prepared for sacrifices and to perform deeds of velour and dedication for our beloved country."

He himself was a veteran of World War II and the 1962 War, a soldier par excellence, a leader most courageous, shrewd and pragmatic.

On 9th, the Commander had asked Anant to accompany him to the Divisional Headquarters. As it happened, the Corps Commander was also present there along with the Divisional Commander. The Corps Commander expressed his dissatisfaction on the tardy advance, and commanded for early capture of Barki. There was silence for some time, which was broken by Anant. Confident of his Battalion, he volunteered to capture Barki. Then and there, he was promised support of Divisional Artillery and Armoured Regiment. Plans were drawn for a two Battalion attack and a third being reserve. However, Anant requested only his Unit for Barki, which was agreed to.

Besides formidable defense system, Barki had 11 concrete pill boxes, in defense of the village and Ichhogil canal behind it. The pill boxes and four feet-wide walls were so strong that even a direct hit of artillery shell or tank's rocket could not destroy it. Each pillbox was equipped with a medium machine gun, a light machine gun, one or two rifles or sten guns and ample supply of ammunition and grenades. On the left of the road, there was a solid building of police station, which was prepared to locate weapons which could bring heavy volume of fire upon an attacker. A deep ditch was expected before Barki.

The Ichhogil, known in Pakistan as BRBL Canal (Bambawalla Ravi Bedian Link), was made as a defense system in 1950, linking Ravi to Sutlej to defend Lahore. It had pill boxes on it; its rear bank being three feet higher than the front, so as effective fire could be brought to bear upon the attacker from there, too. The tanks could move on the track behind the canal with only turrets and guns up to fire in front. The canal was 150 feet wide and 17 feet deep, filled with water, which could be controlled.

According to the plan, 9 *Madras* was to provide firm base in line with Barka Khurd, on the right of the road. Armour Regiment less two squadrons of *Central India Horse* (CIH), equipped with Sherman tanks, were to assault Barki in an unorthodox role with lights on, firing all its armaments, followed immediately behind by 4 *Sikh* to do physical assault and capture Barki in Phase I of the Brigade attack. Ichhogil canal which was expected to be 500 to 700 yards behind was to be captured by 16 *Punjab* in Phase II.

The *Sikhs* had moved right of the road in the intervening night of September 9 and 10, behind the *Madrasis*. Anant gave his orders to his sub-unit Commanders on 10th, setting the mood for the fight with the following words in Punjabi:

> "It is one of the luckiest days for XXXVI. We are moving back to our 'homes' from where we had been pushed out at the time of Partition. Today Barki is like a bride and we the bridegroom. The elephants (tanks) will lead the marriage procession and crackers and lights (artillery) will put a Diwali celebration to shame. I am confident; XXXVI will live up to its traditions of bravery and sacrifices."

The plan in the Unit was that Shamsher's 'A' Company and Subedar Sadhu Singh's 'C' Company would be the assault companies with Dalip's 'B' Company being in reserve. Lieutenant Hari Singh with medium machine gun component was to assault alongwith 'C' Company. The assault was on the right side of the road.

Kanwal's 'D' Company was assigned a special task to move behind the tanks in civilian trucks full of wooden planks to be lowered into the Barki drain so as tanks could cross it. In this 100 per cent casualties were acceptable. And on success of this task, Company was to capture police station area left of the road and reorganize there.

The assault Companies formed up for attack without the firm base since the *Madrasis* had moved back under heavy enemy fire. The assault Compnies formed up at the Start Line at 7.50 pm, but was pounded by the enemy heavily since a registered target, hence they moved forward by 200 yards. Kanwal's Company was waiting for tanks at the appointed rendezvous, Mile 16, at 7.30 pm, the fixed time. Armour did not fetch up. But as he was sure that tanks would be coming, Anant ordered the assault Companies to move at 8 pm, the Start Time.

Artillery started pounding enemy positions, though lesser in scale than planned, probably due to some other priorities. The faulty setting of enemy medium machine guns on fixed lines, at a range of 1,500-2,000 yards, helped attacking troops march underneath the trajectories. It was a sight worth watching with a deadly web of hundreds of whistling bullets with orange tracers, criss crossing, and a heavy barrage of enemy bombs landing all around with piercing shrieks and bursts. The enemy illuminated the entire area turning it into daylight. This enhanced the speed of attack to reach the objective as fast as possible.

Kanwal heard Shamsher repeatedly asking Anant as to why the *'bhaibands'* (tanks) were not leading as per plan; there were no answers. Kanwal was getting impatient waiting at Mile 16, near Barka Kalan for tanks to arrive. There were to and fro calls among Anant, Shamsher, Duggal and Kanwal. Shamsher was also in touch with Sadhu to keep line of attack and to deal with enemy forward detachments. Duggal asked Brigade Headquarters for tanks, but there was no satisfactory answer. Attacking troops started closing in on to pill boxes, from where the fire was now effective. The Battalion mortars brought in heavy shelling onto the enemy positions.

Duggal ultimately, after about 20 minutes of assault having begun, conveyed Anant's message to Kanwal, "*'tank'* or no *'tank'*, each man of XXXVI is a *'tank'*. Move left of the road as planned and complete your task." Kanwal had already heard this communication on the common wireless net and thus had moved his Company at a fast pace.

Kanwal's Company had hardly moved for 15 minutes when the tanks arrived rumbling along, firing towards the objective. The bullets and shells were from behind and thus assaulting troops which were much ahead suffered casualties. Kanwal ran to the closest tank. During the training at the academy, he had only introductory knowledge of tanks, could not locate the phone meant for infantry to communicate with the crew inside. He had just moved ahead of the tank's auxiliary armament, a medium machine gun, that it fired a burst which severed one arm of the unlucky signaler following Kanwal immediately behind. In desperation he mounted the moving tank, knocked at the copula with the butt of his sten gun, making a *'daffedar'* (Non Commissioned Officer) opening the latch, whom he asked to convey to all the tanks not to fire in front and to the right, they could fire to the left only. Contrary to the plan, they had not put on their lights, which at this stage proved to be fortunate for the infantry ahead.

Shamsher and Gurdev's Companies were moving on. The decathlon athlete, Hari had picked up a medium machine gun and was firing from the hip, while his men were carrying the ammunition belts along. The enemy's intense artillery fire was augmented by direct firing weapons and armour from behind Ichhogil canal, pill boxes and fortified positions from some housetops and police station.

The Companies inched forward through fire and move tactics with grit and determination, till they were close to a 100 yards from pill boxes, where they shouted their war cry, *"Bole so Nihal, Sat Sri Akal,"* and pounced upon the enemy, crossing the initial pill boxes, detailed men crawling and lobbing hand grenades through the openings and thus silencing them. The move of forward Companies was in short spurts, using fire and move tactics, grit and determination at its best.

Casualties were surmounting but had to be left unattended. Once the forward crust was pierced, there were some hand to hand fights, bayonets crossing bayonets splitting the belles, with filthiest abuses hurled at each other by the foes. Enemy had been crushed, some paralyzed in their pill-boxes hearing the war cry, *"Bole so Nihal, Sat Sri Akal."* Survivals abandoned their positions running helter skelter through the lanes of the village to the safety behind Ichhogil wading through it since the bridge had already been destroyed by them in the evening. 'A' Company neutralized the North-Western portion of the village including the school area up to the road and 'C' Company cleared the North-Eastern area.

The success signal, firing of two para flares, was given by the assault Companies, exactly 70 minutes after the commencement of the attack. Kanwal's Company attacked the police station area and captured it, Enemy's tanks brought in devastating fire on to the Company from across the Ichhogil which was just 150 yards away. While moving forward, Kanwal had noted anti-tank mines hastily laid by the enemy on both sides of the road; track of a tank was blown up about 200 yards from the police station.

Anant asked Kanwal to immediately pass on a message to the armoured not to leave the road or move forward as the objective had already been captured and there was no ditch as such to be crossed. While this message was being passed, Commanding Officer, CIH, Lieutenant Colonel SC Joshi, on a Rcl jeep of 4 *Sikh*, came rushing along on the road and was blown off near the police station, about 25 yards from Kanwal. The brave officer was wounded and succumbed to his injuries later.

The assaulting Companies found Ichhogil only 250 to 300 yards from Barki, contrary to the earlier information of it being about 600 yards away. The defeated enemy had already fled to the rear of the canal; hence in reorganization stage the troops secured the Eastern bank. Shamsher had been wounded and thus was evacuated. Duggal was wounded when he brought the Battalion Headquarters forward and thus was also evacuated.

The task to be done by 16 *Punjab* in Phase II thus was completed in Phase I of the Brigade attack, within two hours of the assault. Enemy's artillery kept on engaging the village throughout the night.

Later, it came to be known that Pakistanis had fired over 3,000 bombs within half an hour to defeat the attack. Major Aziz Bhatti, who had been tasked to defend the formidable defenses of Barki and Ichhogil with two Companies plus, was awarded Pakistan's highest gallantry award, Nisan-I-Haidar, posthumously. 4 *Sikh* had 39 killed and 121 wounded. Battle Honour 'Barki' was awarded to the Unit besides gallantry medals to some personnel.

At dawn, Anant visited Kanwal's Company. He took Kanwal along to show him the other Companies. Since enemy fire was active, they moved cautiously, behind the houses or trees. While reaching the highest building in

Barki which was three-storied and had the enemy command post, Anant was called back to the Divisional Headquarters for another task in some other sector. He left Kanwal at the Battalion Headquarters where Lieutenant BS Chahal, the Signal Officer, was officiating as Adjutant in place of Duggal. Chahal had just silenced a bunker in which a Pak JCO with a soldier were firing around haphazardly and creating nuisance.

While both the officers were sitting in a trench behind a pill box, well protected from the direct enemy fire, Lieutenant Colonel JS Bhullar, CO, 16 *Punjab* reached there with his protection group, Intelligence Officer and Subedar Major. He spoke to the Brigade Commander informing him about the situation. The Brigade Commander desired to come forward. Enemy's two Saber aircraft strafed the location making all duck down. Bhullar dissuaded the Commander from coming forward describing the situation grave. His Battalion was then given the task of moving further north of Barki and secure portions of Ichhogil.

Kanwal asked for water. When offered, he found the taste different; he noticed that the water was reddish. When he inquired about it, he was shown the source to be the village pond in which bodies of all sorts were lying about. In the last five days troops had to drink water from paddy fields quite often. Food and water was brought forward from the rear but distribution was difficult. Food was missed at times. Only lucky ones could manage a nap.

All were tired, hungry, thirsty and filthy; since there had virtually been no respite for the Battalion from 5th to 11th September. But they had made history. Glory had been achieved, though with sacrifices. One of the best attacks of 1965, a set piece, had been accomplished successfully under the finest leadership of Anant. In spite of heavy casualties, morale was sky high, as the brave had reached their 'homes'.

The superb attack by 4 *Sikh* was well rewarded when Dr. S Radhakrishnan, President of India, visited Barki later, had tea with the troops and highly complimented the Battalion for its sacrifices and victory.

Sketch-4

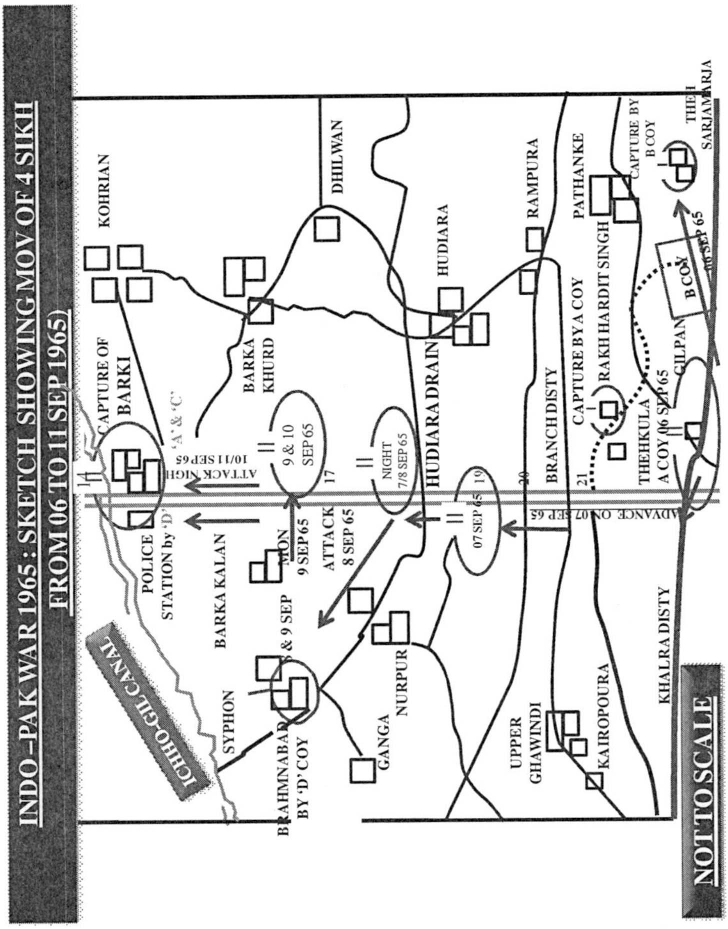
INDO–PAK WAR 1965 : SKETCH SHOWING MOV OF 4 SIKH
FROM 06 TO 11 SEP 1965)
ICHHO-GIL CANAL
NOT TO SCALE
KOHRIAN
CAPTURE OF BARKI
'A' & 'C'
ATTACK NIGHT 10/11 SEP 65
POLICE STATION by 'D'
BARKA KALAN
SYPHON
BRAHMNABAD BY 'D' COY
& 9 SEP
BARKA KHURD
9 & 10 SEP 65
MON 9 SEP 65
ATTACK 8 SEP 65
NIGHT 7/8 SEP 65
17
DHILWAN
GANGA
NURPUR
HUDIARA
HUDIARA DRAIN
07 SEP 65
19
20
UPPER GHAWINDI
RAMPURA
BRANCH DISTY
21
ADVANCE ON 07 SEP 65
KAIROPOURA
PATHANKE
CAPTURE BY A COY
RAKH HARDIT SINGH
THEHKULA
A COY 06 SEP 65
KHALRA DISTY
CAPTURE BY B COY
B COY
06 SEP 65
GILPAN
THEH SARJAMARJA

Sketch-5

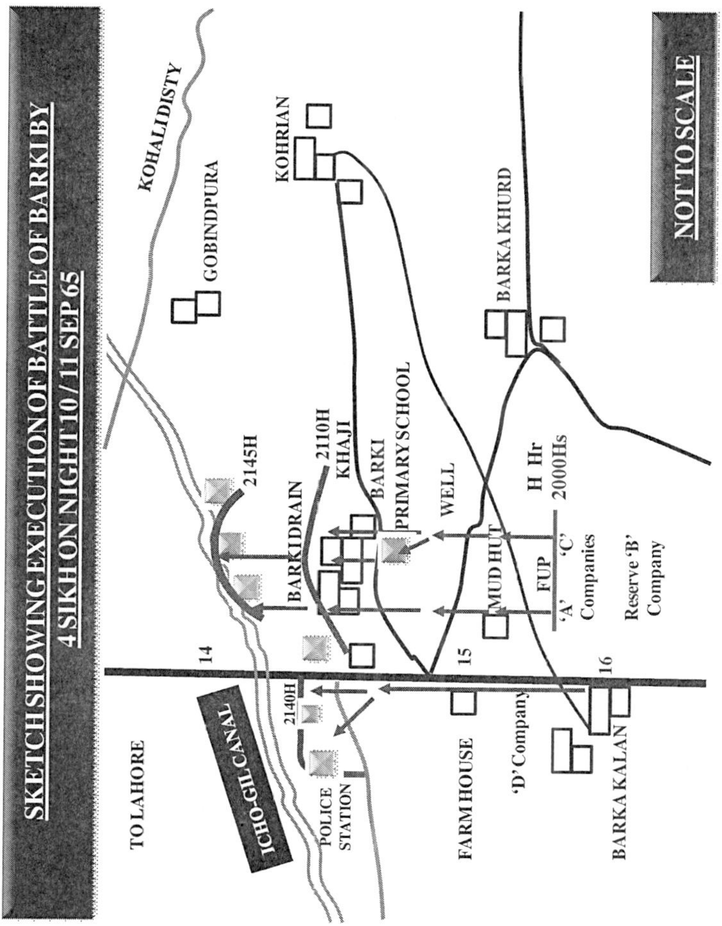
SKETCH SHOWING EXECUTION OF BATTLE OF BARKI BY
4 SIKH ON NIGHT 10/11 SEP 65
NOT TO SCALE
KOHALI DISTY
GOBINDPURA
KOHRIAN
BARKA KHURD
TO LAHORE
ICHO-GIL CANAL
14
2145H
BARKI DRAIN
2110H
KHAJI
BARKI
PRIMARY SCHOOL
WELL
H Hr
2000Hs
MUD HUT
FUP
'A' 'C'
Companies
Reserve 'B'
Company
15
16
2140H
POLICE
STATION
FARM HOUSE
'D' Company
BARKA KALAN

A GALLANT EPISODE

(Sketch 6 enclosed)

4 *Sikh* had captured the formidable Barki defence system against heavy odds, in spite of non-availability of the support, which had been allotted in the plan. The assault was to be by armour, which since was late in reaching at the designated place, the infantry took it on and successfully completed the task, armour reaching the scene only after the success signal was given. The Unit had also bitten more than it was tasked, that is securing the Ichhogil which as per plan was to be captured by another Battalion.

At 8 am, when Lieutenant Colonel Anant Singh, CO was in the process of taking stock of the situation against continuous artillery firing at night and all types of fire, including air strikes since dawn, he was called back to the Division Headquarters, about nine kilometers in the rear. He met the Division Commander who told him that he was required by the Army Commander somewhere further in the rear, for an important mission in another sector.

Anant submitted to the Division Commander that his Battalion had launched a major attack the previous night suffering numerous casualties. He requested that he would like to take stock of the situation and the Battalion be given rest and recuperation. Getting no response, he went to meet the Army Commander. The Corps Commander and another Major General were also present there.

The Army Commander happened to be the Colonel of the Regiment to which the Battalion belonged, himself one of the finest field Commanders Indian army had ever had. There was tremendous appreciation for the excellent job done by the Battalion and it was hoped that the Unit will bag many gallantry awards. The Army Commander told the CO, "I have decided to give you another important task in Valtoha-Khemkaran-Kasur Sector. Further orders and instructions shall be given to you by the Division Commander here under whom the next task shall be carried out. I shall personally come to you on 12th September, on your Battalion's Battle Honour Day, when you would have added another chapter to your glorious record."

Anant sent a message to the Unit at 11.30 am to leave the present position and move back. The relieving Battalion was delayed and thus the Unit was asked to leave the only– previous–night captured Barki and surroundings, and move for another task.

Though tired, the troops walked for almost 10 kilometers where they were provided a hot meal; Lieutenaut PPS Virk, the Quarter Master himself ensuring 'welcome and warmth'. After being in the battle continuously for over 36 hours; the Battalion was transported for 40 kilometers close to Valtoha, reaching there at 10.30 pm on the night of 11-12th September.

Meanwhile, Anant reached the new Division Headquarters at about 4 pm. There was hectic activity in the Headquarters, coordinating plan to capture Kasur in Pakistan. At 5 pm, the General briefed the CO, "The Pakistanis have suffered a defeat and are on the run. Their armour has either been destroyed or gone back. There are only minor pockets of enemy infantry, left immediately opposite us. You will establish a road block in the township of Khemkaran to trap the enemy who may try to run away when one of my Brigades shall be launching an attack supported by armour at dawn and shall link up with you by 8 am on 12th September positively." Khemkaran was five kilometers short of the border, while Kasur was five kilometers west of the border.

The special task involved moving on foot, cross country, for a long distance of 18 kilometers, in an unfamiliar area, capturing a weakly held position and establishing a road block by 6 am on 12th September. 4 Mountain Division, fully embroiled in an intensive battle, after link up with the Battalion, was to continue advance to the prestigious objective of Kasur, in enemy's territory. The information given about the enemy at the road block site was that it was occupied by a weak Company without any armour support. The site was Khemkaran, an Indian township along the border which had been captured by the enemy a few days earlier. But a Pakistani captain who had been captured two nights ago had revealed that the enemy had denuded the position to employ their forces in another sector. Anant told the Division Commander, that the task involved tremendous risks and should be undertaken only after detailed reconnaissance. He also told the General about the operations already undertaken by his Battalion. His representation cut no ice. The quick spate of events, assurances given by senior Commanders, possibility of another achievement and to do a soldier's duty prompted the CO to take on the new mission with full zeal.

The CO was able to get in touch with his Unit by midnight of 11-12th September. He briefed his officers and other junior commanders, and then addressed the men. A local Deputy Superintendent Police (DSP) joined to show the route. The Unit started for its objective immediately. Though the higher echelons had assured that there were no tanks, Anant decided to manhandle two recoil-less guns, each weighing 219 kilograms (barrel and tripod) which could destroy a tank. Its heavy ammunition was distributed among the men of a rifle Company. But as the Unit reached midway, it was realized that the column was becoming unwieldy and thus there were chances of getting late. Anant ordered the heavy guns to be sent back along with some men under Second Lieutenant Gyan Chand. Thereafter, the move was fast as they were being guided by a couple of men belonging to that area since the DSP had vanished from the scene.

Enroute the Unit's forward elements were challenged by an enemy's patrol, but in requirement of speed, the men abused them and marched past. Surprisingly, the Pakistanis didn't fire and instead ran away, but with vital information. The Unit reached its designated firm base by 4.5 am marching at night in an unreconnoitered area, with enough time to organize its attack. The firm base was on a flank of the objective which was just 600 meters away from Khemkaran and 300 meters from the road Khemkaran-Kasur. It was still dark. The CO was giving last minute instructions to his assaulting Company Commanders, Sidhu and Kanwal, when they heard tank noises from ahead and it appeared that they were moving towards their rear. On the contrary and to the dismay of assaulting troops, two troops of enemy tanks took up positions just 400 meters away in a manner that they could bring effective enfilade fire on to the Battalion. This was an utter surprise. It was felt prudent to wait for a while and watch for their further action.

It was 6 am and battle noises were heard from the direction of Indian troops, moving for link up and then move on into enemy territory. As the enemy tanks had taken up a dominating position, it became difficult for the Unit to make any move towards the objective. But, in the light, it was to some relief that the Unit found itself in a position to dominate the road to Kasur by fire. Since there was hardly any effective weapon available to deal with the enemy tanks, it was decided to consolidate at the present location till either a link up was established or, hopefully, enemy tanks moved off. There were six tanks menacingly positioned.

The Division Headquarters had detailed a Signal Detachment with a radio set for communications to accompany the Unit. But somewhere enroute, as a mystery the Detachment was lost. To add to irony, even the artillery Battery Commander had also extricated himself with his detachment and thus that alternative means of communication was also not available, what to say of the artillery support that was expected of him.

At about 7 am, the enemy's tactical reconnaissance aircraft flew over the Battalion twice and guided its artillery fire on the Battalion. The slit trenches dug up in a short time were no saviour. The Unit was in a precarious situation. Casualties were being suffered. Patrols sent out to see the objective area or to establish link up with own troops did not succeed. One patrol clashed with the enemy and two men were captured by them. The Unit's location was well marked and the enemy started pounding heavily. Time now was 10.30 am.

The Unit's position out in the open was becoming untenable, so the CO ordered to move into the protection of built up area at the objective. As the Unit started moving, the enemy tanks opened up fire from the left flank. Enemy shelling increased, including airbursts. Moving as a Battalion group would have incurred heavy casualties, so the CO ordered the troops to move to the objective area in fanned out smaller groups under the Company control.

While these groups were moving, another enemy troop suddenly appeared from behind the tall elephant grass. It had covered the Unit from the rear and right flank. The enemy tanks on the left also started moving forward and started engaging. The platoons had scattered in an area of three kilometers, some trying to move forward, some watching hidden in elephant grass or sugarcane fields, and some reaching close to the objective to be captured by the overwhelming count of enemy infantry and armour. Sidhu, who was a little to the rear, started stealthily moving back and resorting to a longer detour, was able to get out. The irony was that he was able to move out of battle arena when his CO and the maximum men of his own Company were captured by the enemy, as compared to other Companies.

Efforts to destroy enemy tanks from 30 metres by hand-held weapons by Chahal and Kanwal failed since none out of the three anti-tank grenade firing rifles tried would fire. CO's own group was surrounded by enemy armour at 11.30 am and was led for two kilometers to the rear of township with hands raised. About 100 personnel were rounded off in an area of four square kilometers and taken as prisoners.

20 persons died including a newly commissioned officer, Second Lieutenant Ajit Singh. The Indian armoured troop leader from 9 HORSE, Second Lieutenant TS Shergill, sent for link up was also captured, but only when all of his three tanks were destroyed by the enemy fire or mines.

There were enemy troops all around. Indian prisoners were taken to Khemkaran police station, where mockery was at its extreme when their own aircraft targeted them not knowing who they were hitting. Personal information of the prisoners was noted at the Pak Brigade Headquarters.

Later, it came to light that only two days back, enemy Brigade which had captured Khemkaran and had been withdrawn to attack in Fazilka Sector, had again been brought back with just a Battalion less, that is about 2,000 men in that area. It had a Regiment of armour less one Squadron that had about 30 tanks in support, the biggest bugbear for foot soldiers in plains. An Indian assault by two Brigades had failed.

The Battalion won some awards for capture of Barki, besides 'Battle Honour' and 'Theatre Honour', but nothing for doing its task at Khemkaran. The CO who had led four important attacks got no award, not even a promotion. Only one Company Commander out of the four who captured Barki got an award. Some senior commanders got sacked for failure to capture Khemkaran; commanders senior to them got gallantry awards which were supposed to be given to those who depicted bravery in the face of enemy. The Company Commander who had been able to move out of the enemy net, was found to be a suitable alibi to the higher commanders' version of the outcome of their gamble which was "so well intentioned" but had failed.

Some, unfortunately, played on Pakistan's propaganda, and had the audacity of calling it 'surrender', linking it up with the religious-political agitation of that time by Sikhs for Punjabi *Suba* in the Indian state of Punjab. An audacious adventure planned on imperfect intelligence and a failed link up by a large force, resulted in a scurrilous end to such a gallant episode.

Sketch-6: Sketch Showing Indo-Pak Area of 4 Sikh Operations-1965

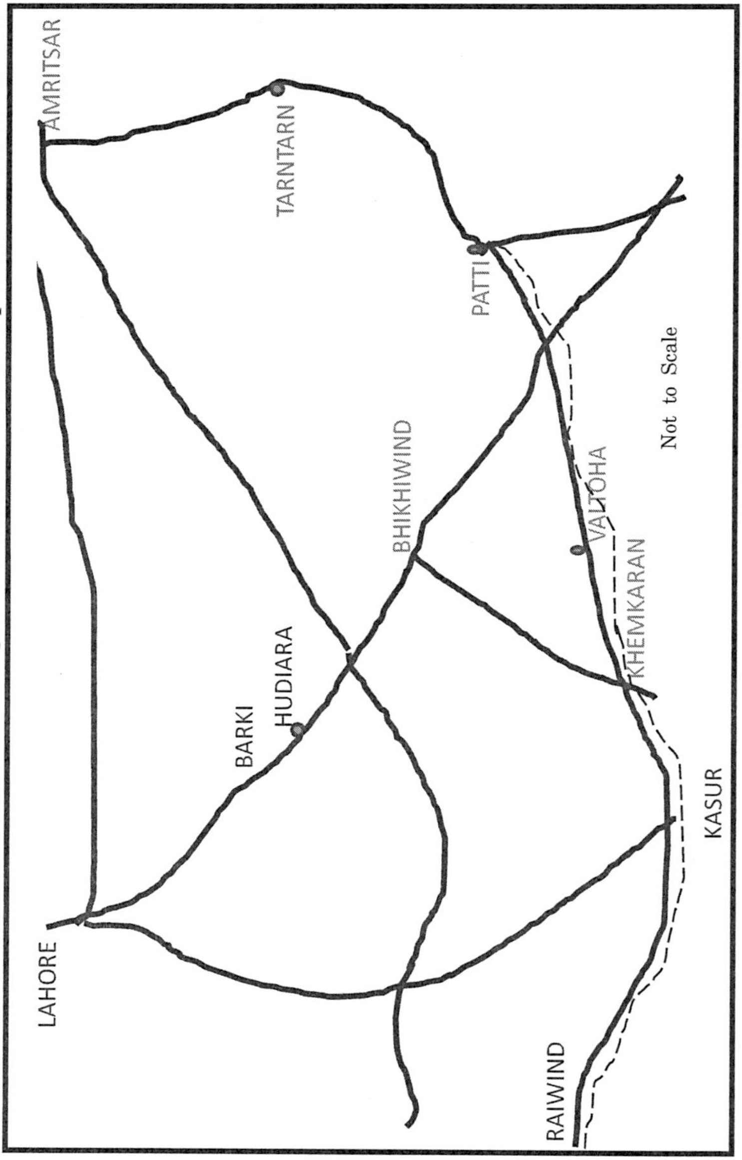

6

Duress

PRISONER OF WAR—

LAHORE-RAWALPINDI-KOHAT

The 1965 Indo-Pak War was the first real test for the Indian and Pakistan forces. Earlier, the troops of both sides had served together on many excursions including World Wars I and II. They knew their mettle.

The troops of the two countries, who till yesterday were brothers-in-arms had become bitter foes after partition, and that too deadly. It was a war where some of the senior commanders were also put to test. The overall overcome was certainly a shade better for Indian forces. The Western powers prevailed upon the political leadership of both the countries, besides a weakening logistic support on both the sides, to stop the hostilities.

The ferociousness with which both the countries pounced upon each other, had started petering out and instead of further venturing deep into other's territory, the built-up euphoria had been replaced by an effort to consolidate on what had been gained and an inert wish to conclude as soon as possible. A prolonged war would have entailed tremendous resources, political will power and external support which, by that time had either dwindled or was not forthcoming.

The truth and irony of war between nations in which soldiers killed soldiers, soon became a thing of the past, though skeptically. The innate warmth and respect between opposing forces, facing each other eyeball to eyeball transformed into grins, salutations and goodwill gestures to each other at the very places they had shed blood. Weekly or as and when required meetings along the International border led to foes-becoming-friends, at least outwardly. If Indians presented liquor to their counterparts, in return they were offered the best of dry fruits.

Lieutenant Colonel Anant Singh, along with five officers and over a hundred men was captured spread out in area of about three square kilometers while attempting to reach Khemkaran. There were a number of troops from some other units also in the Police Station area. Kanwal, who had suffered a minor injury on his left shoulder due to a split up bullet, ricocheted after hitting the railway line, was also in the net. He had been captured along with his CO and officiating Adjutant, Lieutenant Chahal. He noticed some Indian civilians, too, rounded up. Soon military trucks arrived there. The officer prisoners were blindfolded, hand-cuffed in their backs, bundled into the trucks and their hands were tied to the truck railings. The Pakistani soldiers with guns ready guarded them. The soldiers were made to walk.

After travelling for some time, Kanwal heard shouts and abuses all around. From the talk of Pak soldiers, Kanwal could make out that they were crossing through Kasur. The trucks were stopped about 15 kilometers short of Lahore at their Rear Divisional Headquarters. The prisoners of war were given a cup of tea, and were interviewed by a Pak Lieutenant Colonel and a Major. They sought for not only personal information of individuals, but also about location of armour and Sikh troops. They were totally confused by what they were told by the men of 4 *Sikh*. Some soldiers had gone on leave from Rupa (erstwhile NEFA), and joined the Unit just before or during the hostilities. At Rupa, the Unit was a part of 11 Mountain Brigade (of 2 Mountain Division), on loan to 5 Mountain Division. They wore Formation Sign of '*two dahs*' on their shoulders, while troops of 5 Mountain Division had '*red ball*' on their Formation Signs. To capture Barki, as part of 7 Infantry Division, Unit wore the '*arrow*' sign; and the very next day they were attacking Khemkaran as a part of 4 Mountain Division with a different Formation Sign. The Pakistani perplexed minds were at cross-roads to understand about a 'special task force' that India had created in which a unit could be in the North of the country in Tirap Division, then in Kameng, and no sooner in war in the West, fight a major action, and still had the wherewithal to launch yet a special mission of establishing a road-block in a separate sector.

The prisoners were once again mustered into trucks and taken to a newly built Civil Jail at Lahore. The officers were shown separate small cells, meant for those convicted for murder or such heinous crimes, liable to be hanged or given life imprisonment. All slept on the ground. Food was given through a small gap under the iron rods into a shallow plate – two badly cooked chapattis and waterish '*dal*'. Used earthen pots were available for water. There was a drain from one cell to the other, meant for toilet. Water was rushed through it once each in the morning and evening. In-between, soil remained in the drain. Kanwal had drank water from the sugarcane fields and once from a pond at Barki, enough to churn up his guts to a steady relief at night a number of times.

Kanwal thought, 'what a fate of soldiers who deserved honours and awards!' A solitary confinement! Pakistanis couldn't ask for more befitting inauguration of their new jail. Kanwal was awakened four times during the night and dragged twice to an office for interrogation. So was the fate of all the officers.

Early next morning, officers, JCOs and some soldiers were taken out of their cells into the open area of the Jail.

The CO was suddenly embraced by a Pakistani Junior Commissioned Officer, claiming rightly that they had served together in *Punjab* Regiment before the partition. He also mentioned that he had attended Anant's marriage and had sung Punjabi songs to the amusement and appreciation of all. The incident brought smiles on some faces. A number of photographs were taken of the prisoners with Pak troops and some foreign press reporters all around.

The intrinsic irony of the incident was highly exploited by Pakistan, full advantage was taken and in no time media was full of photographs with flimsy write ups in newspapers, radio and televisions in the Western countries; especially Daily Telegraph London published the photograph of Pakistani JCO embracing Anant, with the caption, "Sikhs don't want to fight." Taking up the 1964-65 agitation by the Sikh religious and political leaders for a separate state of *Punjabi Suba*– though the mainstream only wanted some privileges – Pakistani propaganda had become frenzied that even the Sikh soldiers wanted the same. They even went to the extent of saying that the Indian officers had voluntarily surrendered along with Sikh soldiers and had shunned fighting with Pakistan. They said all this despite fully knowing that they were referring to the same troops who had captured Barki, one of Pakistan's most formidable positions only two days back, giving them a mighty blow.

But the ploy did work in the minds of those ignorant of the reality. A joke well exploited, scruples thrown to the wind, but it remained butt of a joke as none fell in the trap.

The following journey was almost for the whole day, in civilian buses painted distastefully, crudely built, uncomfortable seats, window glasses closed and hurriedly painted black. These moved fast avoiding pelting of stones by the people at villages and towns. Kanwal was able to have flying glimpses through his loosely tied blindfold and the front glass which obviously was not painted black. The villages were mud houses, towns dirty littered with cow dung, detestable festoons and crowded with unkempt people.

Outskirts of Rawalpindi were clean and picturesque. They were taken to the cantonment area and swarmed into barracks, all secured with barbed wire all around. Kanwal was with few other officers, including Lieutenants Chahal and Hari Singh, and Second Lieutenant Grewal of the same Battalion. There was also present Captain Harcharan Singh (Doctor with 4 *Sikh*). Cots and beds were provided. They were kept there for four days, primarily for detailed interrogation. The CO was interrogated almost all the days and was grilled thoroughly. He was grim and stressed all the time, not wanting any conversation.

Some civilian prisoners were seen, couple of them in late 80s, one totally blind. Purpose of having such prisoners was not understood and it was disgusting to comprehend if captured to depict a large count.

The prisoners of war, as was known later, were kept mainly in two camps at Kohat and Dargai, in North-West Frontier Area. These were the forts constructed during the reign of Maharaja Ranjit Singh, later improved by the British, to control the Pathan tribes and keep routes to Afghanistan secured. One group of prisoners was taken to Kohat in an old meter-gauge train that had bogies institutionalised during 1942 to ferry the political masses agitating for 'Quit India' movement.

A bogey had several partitions divided by iron rods. There were rickety wooden benches, nailed to the floors or sides. Six persons could be accommodated in one such segment. On the sides of these segments, there were better furnished portions where the guards were accommodated to keep control of the prisoners. In one of such segments where Kanwal was thrust into, there were a total of thirteen – all packed like sardines – sitting, crouching and lying with their limbs on somebody or the other. Relieving a tired limb or back drew curse from the affected two or three. All had to be careful for an amputee, whose leg had been severed from above the knee and the cut portion was still oozing out blood. He was in dire pain and crying. There was yet another prisoner who was shivering with high fever.

Kanwal lied down on the floor with legs under the bench, torso twitched along the bathroom wall and his head just short of the bathroom door. The stink was nostalgic. After a while when he touched his turban, he found it wet with the faeces which had seeped out from under the door. The train moved at night so as there was no trouble from the civilians—so was understood from the talk of the guards. All the railway stations had been blacked out. The horrendous journey was for 19 hours, without food or water. At the destination railway station, the train doors were opened; prisoners detrained, blindfolded tightly, handcuffed again, shoved into trucks and were carried to Kohat fort.

Through the blindfold, Kanwal noted the moat without water outside the fort, high outer wall, the bridge, the large door through which the trucks entered and through yet another wall they emerged into an open area. The handcuffs and blindfolds were removed. There were scores of Pak soldiers around, with their weapons in ready position.

All the prisoners of different affiliations were counted for and assigned to rooms in barracks. Anant, Kanwal, Chahal, Hari, Grewal and Shergill were taken to a barrack whose parapet had been secured with concertina and barbed wire. Already, there were six other prisoners there from the Air Force. There were three enclosures in which there were two rooms each. Two offices were accommodated in each room. The prisoners were changed around to other rooms or enclosures every fortnight or so to ensure nobody could team up to escape.

All had a chance to know the circumstances under which they were captured. But one capture baffled all; that of Squadron Leader Sikand who when on a mission to Kohat airfield, when chased by Sabres had landed with his Knat intact instead of bailing out, thus ensuring his aircraft destroyed. The officer prisoners used to see maneuvers like dogfight or scissors, besides chasing and ducking between the Knat and other Pakistani aircraft trying to know the versatility of the 'small, naughty and dreaded' little bird, notwithstanding the skilled and motivated Indian pilots.

Somehow, Kanwal and Mao Shergill were in the same room for almost a month. Spirited Shergill traded his gold ring which he had been able to hide, and procured a knife-blade from somewhere. For days, while Kanwal kept the vigil, Shergill slowly and slowly loosened two bricks in the roof, which was low to reach when approached with a T-poy adjusted on the cot. Shergill inserted his head through the hole, was looking around in a bid to find some way to escape, when a guard came by on the roof as part of his vigil. Shergill closed the hole quickly. They kept up their efforts for two days more, which failed since they were moved to different rooms as a routine.

The living conditions were horrible. For almost two months, they had only one pair each of trousers and shirts. The prisoners purchased one thin quilt, two bed sheets and a pillow from the peltry Rs. 47 per month that was due to them as per Geneva Convention. Because of the hills all around the cold was severe. The blizzards brought heavy showers and fast cold winds.

Prisoners purchased articles of necessity like toothbrushes, pastes, and soaps etcetera. Most of the articles were gifted by China or Japan. A petty thing like a notebook or a pen was gifted by USA. A pack of cards or a playing ring, though gifts had to be purchased. All were given at double the rates. Food was at its worst. Rotten lady fingers, pumpkin or a little of *dal* was thrown into boiling water—chilly and salt at the whim of the cook. All requests to improve food and tea fell on deaf ears—Geneva Convention flouted.

The Camp Commandant was a re-employed Major who hated even the fallen soldiers. Sentries openly abused, thumped their feet on the roof, and intentionally did coughing, hiccupping or sneezing to disturb or tease.

It was interesting that Pakistani interrogation staff always asked two questions repeatedly: where were Indian armour and Sikh troops deployed; the latter because they wanted to throw leaflets to them convincing them to surrender and that Pakistan will help in every possible manner to achieve their political aim. They had been doing so wherever they had scanty information. What a pity that they succeeded nowhere!

On the same grounds interviews were held with other prisoners of war, especially Sikh personnel. One such interview would be of interest.

Professor Bukhari, who was credited for pioneering Pakistan Radio from Lahore and who was also the Head of UN Information Department in New York, interviewed Kanwal.

Bukhari: "Well Kanwal, I have gone through your previous reports. (The information was perhaps based on their interviews of the men captured). I am happy to see the soldier traits displayed by you."

Kanwal looked at Bukhari innocently and amusingly. He smirked, "Sir, You would have found the same with all of us."

Bukhari: "But I notice you are rather proud. At times foolish. We are treating you well. But you people are not trying to understand. Look at the poverty in your country. Only Punjab has something to speak off where the Sikhs are being exploited. We know people have to eat leaves in other states in order to survive."

Kanwal: "You know better. But I do not know leaves of which trees you are talking about. Though in Pakistan, as per the Geneva Convention, we as prisoners of war are not being given food that is due to us, besides asking for double the price of articles gifted by other countries."

Anger showed on the face of Bukhari, who had been selected to motivate the Sikhs to become turncoats through his convincing skills and Punjabi background. His large ears with hair protruding out turned red to see such daring nonsense of a lieutenant – a bloody prisoner who ought to be kicked on his butt, and thrown into a gutter like a mouse caught in a cage, drowned in water, thrown out, slithering before dying, only to be ignored with disdain. But then he was Bukhari, a great name in Pakistan; how could he be annoyed with a stupid man? He had a mission. He advised, cajoled, subterfuged, and threatened.

Coming to an end, Bukhari said, "I am happy to note that you are after all an intelligent fellow and have understood all that I have been telling you. You are like my son. I wish you grow in life. We love Sikhs. We were together in Maharaja Ranjit Singh's kingdom who had been one of the greatest. We must have the same bonds again. Do you understand what I am trying to tell you?"

Kanwal: "Yes sir."

Bukhari: "My son, I give you a choice to embrace Pakistan till you attain a homeland for yourself for which your great leaders are making sacrifices. One day too soon it will be there. *In-Sha-Allah.* Pakistan is helping you. So, I beseech you to openly express yourself to adopt Pakistan as your country in exile."

Kanwal was totally confused of harangue bombarded upon him for over last two hours. Ultimately he gathered his wits and courage and coyly asked, "Sir, I accept all that you have offered. I shall stay in Pakistan if allowed four wives as per your law."

The next day, all over the media, it was flashed, "Sir, I accept all that you have offered."

Bukhari was satisfied that his government had recognized his efforts. But it never became clear why he never returned to try his convincing abilities.

Kanwal's interview proved to be a blessing in disguise. A distant relative in the USA saw the news on the television, and immediately rang up Kanwal's father saying Kanwal might be changing his religion. Kanwal's relatives heaved a sigh of relief but not without certain misgivings. Some even felt what was so "happy" about this news when a person was living as a body but without a soul. Kanwal's father, a Veteran of World War, knew his naughty son, and remarked, "Our gratitude to Almighty God, Kanwal is alive. We shall see him soon."

After about two and half months, there was some major shuffling around. Most of the prisoners were moved to Dargai.

PRISONER OF WAR AT DARGAI AND REPATRIATION

Dargai Fort was located in the Khanki Valley of NWFA. Irony was that the soldiers of 4 *Sikh* could see the hills where their predecessors had fought the famous Battle of Saragarhi in 1897, where 21 brave martyrs had fought against a large *lashkar* of 20,000 Arakazais and Afridis. All 21 were awarded Indian Order of Merit posthumously, the then highest award given to Indians, today equivalent to Param Vir Chakra. The British Parliament had given a standing ovation to this outstanding display of bravery, sacrifice and patriotism; besides many other awards in cash and land.

Dargai was the main prisoners' camp. The men were kept as per their groups i.e. Gurkhas, South Indians, Sikhs and others, primarily from administrative point of view. For officers, there were three cages, each separated by a seven feet high wall. In one, they kept all Air Force officers, in the next Sikhs and in the last one the rest. There was no difference in the treatment of one group from the other. It was easy to win over a generous sentry or hoodwink him and talk to the officers next door. Letters were sneaked through to each other through the drain or wrapped around a pebble and thrown over the wall.

The overall treatment was better here. It must go to the credit of an affable and considerate Lieutenant Colonel Akram and his suave and generous Deputy, Major Quereshi.

There used to be discussions with them at times sharing views on various political, religious and social issues in both the countries. If they said something unacceptable, they were paid in the same coin. They accepted the outbursts of prisoners with understanding. They escorted officers to the men's cages on Birthday celebrations of Guru Nanak Dev. There were warm hugs and moist eyes. Many Pak civilians and families used to come and see prisoners. They used to be highly amused to see the prisoners in large size shirts, trousers or shorts with big letters PW printed in black on their clothes. There could not be any interaction with them. But once on a visit along with his family, Major Quereshi had sent his six-year old daughter inside the cage. Chahal played marbles with the chubby child. She was so taken in by so many prisoner 'uncles' showering their blessings. All the prisoners, though in relatively improved living conditions started missing their country and families much more than earlier days of captivity.

Food was now cooked by their own men and hence quality was much better though quantity yet limited. Some clothing was provided through Indian Red Cross with kind offices of UNO. Since the prisoners had procured their daily necessities, they now pooled money to buy odd fruit, vegetable, tea leaves or other eatables like groundnuts and jaggery.

By January 1966, gifts and letters were received from home. There was a small packet of resins for each prisoner from that time heart throb-actress Asha Parekh. Each piece was relished by many till repatriation in February. There was sufficient to eat and little more satisfaction. The prisoners played cards and ring to keep busy. However, despite requests, no newspapers or books were provided. Regular prayers in the morning and evening were a solace. After several requests, the Pak authorities permitted Kanwal and Chahal to learn Urdu from Grewal.

Finally, Tashkent talks succeeded, and prisoners were repatriated to their own countries. The exchange took place at Husainiwala Border at Ferozepur. Indian prisoners carried their beds on their heads with bags hung on their shoulders. They all were weak and thin. All were made to stand in a queue. Pak prisoner soldiers were in a queue on the other side of the border. All were well nourished, wore ironed clean uniforms and were carrying transistors and cameras. Officers' baggage perhaps was being carried by their men. That was for India following the Geneva Convention explicitly. One step before crossing the border line, Kanwal hurled back the bedding carrying clothes with writ large the word PW, and crossed the border. Others carried their stuff as a memory.

The repatriated soldiers were given a hearty welcome by Services officers. Kanwal's parents, helped by Lieutenant Colonel Shamsher Singh, CO, 4 *Sikh*, were able to meet their son and other officers. Anant had a hot dialogue with the GOC, 7 Infantry Division (the communication is kept out of the preview of this book intentionally).

Most of the officers were taken to Mathura for debriefing awaiting their postings to various places. It was during this time that relatives of many personnel dead or missing came to ask the repatriated soldiers information about their 'own'. Widowed, expecting wife of martyr Second Lieutenant Ajit Singh vowed that if she got a son she will send him to 4 *Sikh* (which she did).

7

Convalescence

'BULADA' IN BOXING RING

Gurcharan *'bulada'* was tall, lean but muscular, with long flailing arms ending into thick strong hands. If he took off his shirt, his six-pack body with prominent sinews, showed off in various sizes of bulging knots. He had moustache trimmed and armpits shaved. His forehead had a diagonal gash about two inches long which somehow added to his rugged handsomeness.

A man of few words, but each sentence punctured with a real Punjabi abuse whenever required, grating through clenched teeth, at times just a hiss. Called *'Bulada'* or *'budlada'* because he belonged to Bathinda district in Punjab known for its virility, rough sense of pride and plenty of boorishness, with negligible education way back in 1960s, and hence a name as given to all studs in the district. He was out-rightly the best boxer in the Unit famous for its excellent boxing team, who played the sport scientifically with the best techniques. He himself had represented the Services in the Nationals several times, never going beyond more for his demeanour than boxing prowess.

Another Unit in Station also had the place of pride in sports, wherever they went. The competition in the Station was thus mostly in these Units, for the sake of interest, let us name them the Sikhs and Punjabis. The Sikhs were decisively doing better much to the envy of the other to the extent that several situations turned ugly.

By the final day, four fights had gone in favour of the Sikhs, two in favour of the Punjabis and one for the

Madrasis. The ninth fight was between the boxers of the two main antagonists, which was a rather bitter struggle. Somehow the referee gave an erroneous decision and the Sikhs lost the fight on points. Two fights were left, two boxers from the Sikhs and one each from the other two units.

The last but one fight was between Gurcharan Havildar of the the Sikhs and Tuke Ram Havildar of the Punjabis. Tuke was also a renowned boxer and perhaps the best of the Punjabis. It was the most awaited fight of the day. Red and blue corners announced, the referee made them shake their hands and part to their corners, Tuke giving a harsh look at *'bulada'*.

On sounding the gong, both moved into the arena and started prancing about in a circular fashion. Tuke looked ferocious with red shot eyes and a jaunty caricature. He showed the anger for seemingly losing the overall competition. Gurcharan looked calm and composed and nobody could fathom what was going on in his mind, except a few who knew the turmoil raging within him to avenge the last defeat which according to him was unjustified. There was no doubt in his mind that this fight had to be a knock out.

Not yet getting into the mode of hitting each other, the referee gestured them to get engaged which they did with an amazing speed. Tuke's charge was unstoppable with dozens of punches flying about, a few hitting the agile Gurcharan, that also on his gloves. The massive punches could not break the guard of Gurcharan's face, which did open just two or three times by the end of the first round, landing at Gurcharan's jaws.

Second round and Tuke looked terribly dissatisfied not having been able to knock out a petrified opponent trying to avoid a fight. He also knew that the first round had gone in his favour, more because of aggression than skill. He must win the second round also. He landed heavy barrage of punches on Gurcharan's face and stomach. One such massive punch landed squarely on Gurcharan's lips letting out blood. He tasted it; cleaned it with his glove and the glove with his short, and gaining total surprise gave three punches on Tuke's face who reeled back staggering. The referee came to Tuke's rescue and started counting. By 'eight' Tuke was ready.

Without giving any time Gurcharan flew his full throttled left on Tuke's right temple. Tuke Ram's jaws opened, the bait flew out and before the referee could intervene, a right hander had brought out blood gushing from Tuke's lips. He fell like a sawed off tree. 'Towel' was thrown in and he was carried out.

Gurcharan *'bulada'* came into to the center of the ring. The umpire held his right hand up and announced, "Red is the winner." In the din of a great applause, Gurcharan looked towards the Punjabis and shouted, "Bring two."

The last fight was also won by the Sikhs and they declared the overall winner. The best individual boxer's prize went to the indomitable *'budlada'*. Photographs were taken with the Commander, trophy and individual prizes in front. *'budlada'* had been whisked away lest the Commander expressed his annoyance with his outcry in the ring which somewhat resembled Tarzan's victory cry after a kill.

Gurcharan was next day marched to the Commanding Officer, who punished him with a 'reprimand'. To celebrate victory, later in the evening in the *'barakhana'* drinks party, the Commanding Officer embraced him and presented him with a hefty packet with enough currency to buy a fertile buffalo that *'bulada'* had been hinting at.

SHIKAR AT BIR GUGIANA-FARIDKOT

The army at Ferozepur, a cantonment established by the British against Maharaja Ranjit Singh's kingdom, had the famous Unit in 1965-67 which had five or six officers who were keen on hunting, then a sport encouraged, a legacy left behind by the British. Kanwal was the best shot whose first hobby was this sport, a hereditary talent. His

French double barrel was presented to him by his father when he got commissioned.

Kanwal rang up Major Dalip, his senior officer in the Unit, posted as a staff officer in the same Station, "Sir, how about *shikar* in the evening?"

Dalip: "Love to, when, where and of what kind?"

Kanwal: "Sir, my elder brother, a Major, is in Station, a better shot than me. He can be in your jeep while Captain Lali will be in my jeep. We leave at four in the evening. Basically for partridges and if lucky for anything else. We go to Bir Gugiana since plenty of game is there, though we may have to face the ire of Maharaja of Faridkot if found in his estate."

Dalip: "OK, we will have to be careful, responsibility will be yours."

Bir Gugiana was the private hunting ground of Maharaja of Faridkot which ran into several hundred acres. He didn't like anybody venturing into his lands. Many types of wild trees and bushes grew all over except where '*katcha*' narrow roads and tracks were cut for movement, and jungle lanes to control wild fires, which could be disastrous. The jungle was full of partridges, quail and green pigeons as far as winged '*shikar*' were concerned. In the animal category, it had wild boar, blue bulls, rabbits and barking deer. This was besides numerous other types of animals, birds, reptiles and porcupine.

The two jeeps entered the jungle and moved to different roads. Kanwal had shot two partridges and his brother three, all flying. When Kanwal got down to pick up the last shot partridge, suddenly there appeared an open rickety of a Willys jeep, bent on one side due to the uneven load of about 11 men armed with swords and spears. They got down and stood around their jeep.

Their leader: "What are you doing here?"

Lali, who was at the wheel, said, "A bit of drive."

Leader: "You have also shot partridges."

Lali: "Not any meaningfully. Since we are carrying a gun we have fired on one or two."

Leader: "No, you have two guns with you. We have heard sound of another jeep, from where four shots have been fired."

Lali was about to deny it when the other jeep appeared. Kanwal picked up the last shot partridge and put it in the jeep, moved about 10 meters away. He gestured Dalip to move away which they did as fast as they could before the guards could react. They drove to an alternate area where they bagged a few more partridges.

The warden asked Kanwal to move to his jeep, which the latter refused. Both sides gauged what was happening. While warden's men had swords and spears, Lali and Kanwal had loaded guns. Lali had a slight handicap in using the gun since he was behind the wheel, Kanwal had positioned himself well as a deterrent to warden and his men against any endeavour to harm Lali or snatch his gun. Kanwal had placed his gun, menacingly on his shoulder, ready to shoot if required.

The warden did have the courage to slowly close in on to Lali talking while walking and he tried to pick up the partridges lying in the rear of the jeep. Lali told him that he was the son of a well known landlord and an advocate who had good relationship with the Maharaja. He also said that a hunter never gave away his kill to anyone. He continued that still if there were any serious objections from the warden's side, they would move out and would come only with permission next time.

The warden however was not convinced with the rant. He asked for Lali's and Kanwal's full names which he noted down on a paper where he already had the jeep number. He also asked for the names of other two officers, but Lali feigned ignorance claiming they were a different party.

The warden asked Lali to call Kanwal to the jeep, but Kanwal refused to do so till the warden moved back to his jeep. The hefty, tall warden gave a helpless grin through his large moustache and moved away.

The next day, Kanwal was called by his CO and was asked about the incident. Kanwal narrated the entire story to the amusement of the CO who in his hearts of hearts approved of his officer's courage. However, he admonished Kanwal, "There is a personal complaint from the Maharaja to the General Officer Commanding and you are the culprit. Let it be the last time that I get a complaint like this." Kanwal apologized.

Four days later, Kanwal was again summoned by the CO.

CO: "You are in the news again."

Kanwal shuddered: 'My God, how the hell has he come to know of my hunting trip of yesterday evening, though in a different area'.

Kanwal: "Sir?"

CO: "General Officer Commanding has rung up as he has come to know of your successful frequent hunting trips. He desires you to plan and organize a hunting trip for him and his party for ducks and partridges at the confluence of rivers Sutlej and Bias at Hari-ke-Pattan. It will be followed by a picnic lunch where ladies and some guests from Delhi will join later. The picnic arrangement shall not be your headache. But ensure that the birds are plenty and that there is no shortage."

Kanwal: "Sir, since the ladies are also coming, I hope you will be there too, Sir."

CO: "Will you shut up?"

Kanwal: "Sir, may I have your permission to go a day earlier and stay there for the night also to ensure plenty of birds the next day." The CO understood the game plan whereby Kanwal was going to shoot the previous day catering for the 'plenty'. Kanwal got an approving nod.

Kanwal arranged a motor boat from the irrigation department. The General, two Brigadiers, two Ambassadors and Kanwal's boss travelled in it well before daylight, to the confluence of rivers Sutlej and Beas. They got down and moved for half a kilometer through elephant grass slowly, without making any sound. They noticed tiny shacks here and there where villagers brewed country liquor. The stench was awful.

They reached a vantage-point from where they saw thousands of ducks. There were pintails, shovellers, debchicks, gulls, gadwalls and teals. At a distance, through binoculars they also saw geese and redheads. They all closed on stealthily, took up positions and fired together, except Kanwal who fired two rounds when the ducks were flying off, hitting into each other and falling.

The General remarked: "Great. We all fired when ducks were sitting and perhaps got a bird or two each in the spread pellets made. Kanwal fired while ducks were in the air, when birds were all over, each pellet getting a hit. It was a sight to see several ducks falling down. He also kept his word that he always shot flying birds. Well done, Kanwal."

The picnic was a roaring success with songs and dance. And there was 'plenty' of ducks barbeques with 'plenty' of Russian vodka, in the good presence of 'plenty' of elegant ladies.

In an 'At Home' organized by Maharaja of Faridkot, General took Kanwal along since his Aid-de-Cong (ADC) was on leave. Kanwal mentioned to the Maharaja that he belonged to a Battalion of which Maharaja himself was a 'Honorary Colonel'. Kanwal got a green card to Bir Gugiana.

BHINDER AT SARLA POST : POONCH

The Unit was on the North-Eastern side of the Poonch River, occupying the highest hills against Pakistan. Sarla Post was west of the river on the tip of a long ridge line extending upwards. Sarla was with India while the remaining ridge was with Pakistan, with line of control as border in-between, a perpetual bone of contention. Sarla was held by a platoon of about 25 men, a part of Malti Post on the North-Eastern side of the river. Thus the road to Hajipir Pass in Pakistan, famous for its capture by India in 1965, was defended by these two posts. From Malti, the river was 200 yards away and the pebbled width of the river was about 400 yards.

Some of the villages on both the sides were very close to each other; some looked like the same village when seen from a distance and the line of control passing through it. A check was kept by troops on both the sides to stop any ingress by the civilians from one side to the other. The check was violated very often as the villagers had relations on either side. On some happy or sad family occasions the villagers did seek permission from the post commanders to go across which willy nilly used to be given. The human angle was kept in mind though spies or informers took full advantage of the situation.

There were also springs or water holes, from where people took water by crossing the unmarked border. At Sarla Post also, there was a similar situation where a spring was situated on the Indian side, but very close to the Pakistan occupied area. There were three or four scattered huts inhabited by a few people, basically to look after their agricultural fields on the other side. They were taking water from the spring, which was an understandable breach.

A young officer, Bhinder, was deputed as Sarla Post commander. To his surprise and annoyance, Pakistanis were coming to the Indian side to take water. He admonished his immediate subordinate who had been there for the last many months, for allowing such violation of one's own territory. He watched the entire goings on much to his chagrin for one full week, when he decided to do something about it. He asked one of his men to shout at the Pakistanis not to come to the Indian side. The warnings were given for three days with some effect, but not to his satisfaction.

Bhinder was almost on the verge of firing a few shots to scare them away, when he noticed a slender Pakistani girl descending on the spring with a graceful gait, under the weight of an empty shining brass pitcher on her head and a bucket in her hand, wrist covered with glass bangles. The other hand dangled to and fro as if making dancing movements, her bangles shining in the sun. The swaying form of buck-some pulsating bosom, trim waist and rounded hips, tiptoeing on the zigzag path, pulverized Bhinder. What an engrossing sight!

No firing by Bhinder for three days, he only watched the timing and modus operandi of the girl. His fertile mind had given him a brilliant idea which he set to implement. He was proud of his physique, patriotism and courage. The next day, at predawn, fully camouflaged as per the flora around the spring, he cautiously moved down to the spring, huddled himself behind the boulders, and waited for the kill.

The girl came prancing. As she came near the spring, Bhinder started crawling, the girl was totally oblivious to the 'marauding' movement. Bhinder sprang a total surprise, picked up the girl and flung her on his shoulder, deaf to her objections and one or two shrieks; he carried her to his post. The Pakistani post was far away and other villagers, who were either sleeping or scattered in the fields, could not hear her. The soldiers at the Post were amused.

Bhinder dumped the girl in a bunker adjoining to his, which was for guests. She was looked after well. He was kind to the girl. When she innocently inquired about her utensils, Bhinder sent two *jawans* down to recover them. Three Pakistanis approached, begging from the other side, but Bhinder wouldn't listen.

The Pakistani civilians approached their own post that sought a meeting between the Company Commanders. A sudden call from the CO shook up Bhinder from his day-dream.

Bhinder: "Yes sir, what do these Pakistanis think of themselves of not hearing my warnings. I have picked up one of them to teach a lesson."

CO: “Shut up, you bloody fool. I hope you haven't touched the girl?”

Bhinder stammered: “No, no, sir, except for when I carried her up.”

CO: “Son of a rascal. Don't give her anything now to eat or drink except plain water. Bastard, wait till I come there.”

Bhinder: “Sir, I will get some nice *'pakauras'* made for you.” This was followed by a volley of expletives from the CO.

The distance to the post that was normally covered in an hour's time was done in 40 minutes. The CO was literally puffing, his chest heaving up and down, perspiring, but with enough stamina to bestow the choicest of abuses upon Bhinder. He asked the girl time and again if anything had happened to her. When answered with a categorical 'no', he heaved a sigh of relief. He got some rations put in her pitcher and bucket, pleading her not to complain of any cooked up story, and instructed to move to her house. She was also told that they can have water from the spring like before.

A stern warning was given to Bhinder who did not know that a complaint to the UN observers could have been embarrassing for the country. The situation had been sorted out at the local level. Bhinder, for sometime watched the Pakistanis taking Indian waters with great scorn, but soon got into the mode, offering something or the other to the girl, and restraining himself of any misadventure. He was also greatly relieved that the CO accepted the *'pakauras'* and tea on his next visit to the post.

SHOOTING IN A BUNKER

The Sunday afternoon beer session, after morning temple service and an hour or two of work in the Unit, was almost a ritual. The mini Palace of the erstwhile *Wazir* of Raja of Poonch was being utilized as an Officers' Mess. It was located overlooking a large open ground, which, with its natural seating created by the hill slopes gave the appearance of a stadium. Along this was the road, then the beautiful river whose farther side gradually sloped upwards, joining into high hills of Hajipir pass. Poonch, at a height of 4,000 feet, used to become fairly hot during summers. In the beautiful lawns, under a shady tree, surrounded by a bevy of flowers, beer quenched the thirst, often ending into rather plenty guzzled to a 'glad' stage.

It was at about 3 pm that Kanwal after a rather heavy dose and lunch moved to his bunker. The bunker walls were made of mud, roof of bamboos, thatch and mud, and a door and only ventilator of local timber crudely joined to requirement. A wooden cot, rickety chair and a folding table made for the furniture. The entrance to the bathroom was through a narrow corridor, which had niches cut into the wall to keep folded clothes, a stick struck into opposite walls for hangers and a shoe-rack made out of rum boxes. Small powered bulbs provided light in the three sections to include the bathroom with a commode made of whisky boxes, plank and two buckets, always kept full of water by the helper. Since electricity was scarce, two kerosene lanterns were kept ready.

Earlier reports indicated the presence of snakes in the thatched roof; Kanwal had also heard hissing sounds. The hissing used to be more pronounced during summers in the afternoons, since the snakes perhaps could not bear the hot temperature. But it was always said that the snakes did not enter the bunker and mostly crept in or out of the roof from the top only. That was a comfort to know and thus no sooner did Kanwal make into the bunker, he changed into shorts, hit the bed, sweating and snored to a deep slumber.

A sudden crash, smashing of hair oil bottle on the table hitting into the water bottle covered with a glass tumbler, all falling onto the floor with a cluttering sound awakened Kanwal who shivered for a couple of seconds. Soon, he was about to doze off again when he heard shaking of a powder tin. He looked towards the table and in the dark saw a stick lying diagonally from the roof to the table. He stretched forward to remove the stick fallen off from the roof and got hold of it. The stick slithered in his hand. His heart stopped, all faculties awakened with fear as he trembled at the unexpected. He quickly left the stick, bolted upright in the bed banging his head into the roof with full force, feeling no pain. He opened the small ventilator, some light but not enough, so he clambered on his toes to reach the door handle and tried to open it but couldn't, except managing a little slit. He noticed a huge snake curled up under the table.

Beer had vanished in fumes; the unbroken water bottle was providing cool comfort to the snake while Kanwal's throat was dry. The snake moved and placed himself tactically between the door and the bed, after all it had broken the lower layer of the hot roof and moved to cooler regions and now shall not accept any intrusions. Kanwal was in a dilemma, a bit astounded though in full command of himself. He shouted for the sentry through the ventilator to rush to his Company armory and bring his shotgun with a couple of cartridges.

Bang! The shot was taken from five yards. There was a booming sound of a number four cartridge suitable for duck shoot. Mud plaster from the wall scrapped out and flew all over, thick dust mixed with smoke filled up the bunker and the roof shook throwing down mud and thatch. There was a moment's doubt in Kanwal's mind whether the snake was hit or not, though he was confident of his skills. The gun was still ready with the second cartridge. Dust settled in a minute. The snake had been blown into pieces which were taken out and when the pieces available were put into place by a local, and measured to eight feet long, someone remarked that it was one of the real long cobras. There was a sigh of relief that the life of an officer was spared through good luck that the snake had not fallen on him from the roof.

Meanwhile, a local had examined the mouth and the belly of the snake. He declared the snake to be a rat eater. There were of course hundreds of rats in the area.

The roof of the bunker was ripped open. Nothing objectionable was found. A tent was erected for Kanwal for three days while a new roof was laid on the bunker which was restored to its pristine glory.

It became talk of the town how a gallant officer had faced a grim situation and using his wits and courage had challenged and exterminated a deadly snake. The aching boil on his head was now healed. The men made a skit and staged in the Unit get-together. (The script for the skit was written by Kanwal, hence the authenticated version).

CAR IT WAS - UPI-3935

Remember a Fiat 1961 model with its front doors opening outwards, front seat as one, gear rod under the steering, a protruding petrol pipe on the left hind, a funny looking spiraled jack with a protruding rod to be inserted into the side of the car to lift it and a well-rounded sturdy exterior. Though it could be started with an ignition key, but was also provided with a bent handle that could start the engine with one jerk, if fixed into its slot correctly.

The car cost Rupees 12,000/- a piece, gave approximately nine miles (12 kilometers) per gallon, costing 90 paisa each. Almost all cars at that time were fixed with carriers on tops as if that was the fashion. And a necessity for carrying enormous luggage in steel boxes and tied up bundles of jumbo joint families. Ambassador and Landmaster were the only challenge. Vaux Wagons, Mercedes, Chevrolets, Rolls Royce and Hillmans were scarce. It was rarely run at a speed of more than 40 miles per hour, though the claim was up to 80 miles, due to overheating troubles or just an awe of high speed, and also the thin black top roads with sharp fringes that would not allow for taking risks.

Somewhere in 1971, Kanwal drove in his Fiat which he named *'Bakki'* (mare), from his home in a border town in Punjab, where he was on leave, to Mhow in Madhya Pradesh, for a three-month course of instruction. He stayed the night at Delhi. After crossing Agra, *'Bakki'* had a flat tyre in left rear wheel. There, being no space on the road to fix the clumsy jack, Kanwal had to remove his entire luggage from the boot and rear seat to make it light enough for six passers-by who were kind enough to lift the car long enough for Kanwal to change the tyre, which had a big cut. The spare wheel was also a worn out weak tyre. There being no immediate relief available, the car was somehow tugged to Gwalior, where both the bad tyres were changed.

Kanwal was able to start from Gwalior late in the afternoon and by the time he passed through Shivpuri-Guna area, it was dark. This belt was notorious for dacoits of Chambal. He readied his double barrel shotgun and revolver, and maneuvered his *'Bakki'* between any two trucks that suited, moving at their slow speed and resting a couple of times where they stopped.

At one of such places, he went around a barely lit shanty, for a loo-break, and heard abuses laced in ecstasy. Wondering, he returned to be confronted by a middle-aged man who asked for *'baithega'* for Rupees five for either the old or young. The truckers however, had kept the sisters busy. Amused, Kanwal reached Indore at wee hours, to Mhow in an hour, dead tired and sleepy in the otherwise only company of songs on the stereo, light drinks, chips or salted cashew nuts and the random amusing thought of addition to his vocabulary, *'Baithega!'*

On completion of the training, Kanwal decided to move to his duty station Ramgarh in the then Bihar, via Bhopal-Jabalpur-Mugal Sarai and Hazaribagh on the national highway in his versatile *'Bakki'*. His wife and son, six months old, had since joined him, so the car was full to the brim. After crossing Hoshangabad, the tie rod fell somewhere and the car unhinged, went out of control. Fortunately, he was driving at a very low speed while crossing a village and so the car could be stopped in time, avoiding any mishap.

While they had hot 'country' eggs and tea, the village blacksmith did a good job, he heated and beat up one end of an iron peg that was in use for tethering cows, to a thick head, installed it at the tie rod slot and secured it with electricity cables. He charged Rupees three for the job done. He advised Kanwal to move slowly and change the improvisation to original at the next town Narsimhapur. Tie-rod was not available there; hence they pushed on to Jabalpur where they arrived rather late, to an affectionate welcome at Kanwal's elder brother's house.

The car was given for repairs and a complete check up at a workshop, while the two brothers with their families visited the marble rocks and other beautiful locales along the Narmada River. *'Bakki'* was loaded up in the evening and kept in the garage, so as no time was wasted the next day, and they started driving at 4 am for Ramgarh as their destination.

The monsoons were at their peak, a continuous heavy pour reduced visibility to ten yards or so and driving was hazardous. Water puddles, pits and broken sides of the road added to the misery. After a few hours of monotonous slow journey, they received the unwelcome news that the flood water was overflowing the main bridge on Son River at Sasaram-Dehri, by five feet and hence was closed to traffic. Kanwal had to be on duty the next day.

It was 11 am. The suggestion came that if prepared to take some risk, then to take a detour of about 50 miles on a thin road, cross Son upstream over a culvert with less water overflowing, as the tributaries swelled the Son only after the culvert to make it difficult on the main bridge. With no other option, Kanwal took the detour, travelled about 30 miles on a rather better surfaced road, to see a terrible traffic jam. About 50-60 trucks on the road and ahead of them 5-6 stuck up in the slush on the left, tilted, and an equal number coming from the opposite side stuck up, with 70-80 behind them.

About 300 people were spread out all over, planning, gossiping, idling, sleeping and cursing. They were not worried as they had food to eat, trucks to sleep in, toilet area all around and assured pay or commission in their kitty. They could wait for a day or so till either some help came or it dried up sufficiently for movement. How about Kanwal and family? Cake and biscuits wouldn't have satisfied the child. Some *'khalsa'* drivers came to their rescue. They brought fresh milk of buffaloes being taken in a truck, heated it up and gave it to the beleaguered family. They loved and respected the army personnel. They asked Kanwal to move his car into the fields, and then about a dozen of them, half-lifted the car and pushed it for almost a quarter of a mile, hauling it up on the road again. They gave a loud *'jaikara' 'Bole so Nihal, Sat Sri Akal'*. The road was through thereafter till the culvert.

The rain again set in with an intense downpour. The fastest speed of wipers was also grossly inadequate to clean the glass. The mist formed inside came onto the windshield and windows as fast as it was cleaned by Kanwal's wife. The child, though crying at times, mostly remained playful. Kanwal and his wife were enjoying the tension thus created. Water was flowing about two feet above the culvert. Rain had reduced to a drizzle, sky almost clear from the upstream direction.

Kanwal waited for almost two hours for the water to recede to enable the car to wade through. No way. Ultimately, he had to accept the offer of some villagers that they would help in crossing. They advised him not to start the engine. They tied two ropes in front. Six of them pulled the car in front and a dozen balancing and pushing it from the sides and rear. The car wavered downstream but the sturdy villagers in their loin-clothes, body sinews and muscles rippling, wet and heaving, kept moving at a steady speed. The half-submerged car had water inside up to the waists of the couple sitting by the time they had crossed half of the water line.

Water was hitting into the glass on the driver's side and seeping in. Kanwal's wife had picked up the child above her shoulders, with purse dangling from the hand. Kanwal had gripped hard on the steering wheel with one hand, taken out his wallet and put it in his turban.

On the left was a drop of six feet, muddy thick water falling down in a sheet, creating a watery ditch on the surface and gushing up into a wall of foam to flow into a fast current. Uprooted bushes and ripped off branches were all over. At places swirls were formed around the stones. A thought came to Kanwal's mind, what if the car was swept down, how will he open the door or window to sneak out and whom will he try to save – his wife or son? A tragic smile lumbered up on his lips. As they went further, water became shallower and the car moved faster. The young hearts faced the adversity with great dignity. It was like a bond to accept together what was ultimately destined for them, yet the hope to survive the ordeal kept them going strong. All sorts of grim thoughts were kept at bay with prayers on their minds and love for their son.

The car engine had submerged in the water a number of times; the water would have entered the exhaust and other inlets and outlets. Kanwal was already contemplating an overhaul of the engine. But how will he reach his destination in time? On a villager's gesture, God in his mind, eyes closed, he started the engine which whirred and then stopped. Two villagers, turn by turn, worked on the starting handle but the car wouldn't buzz. He decided to give a last try with the ignition key. The engine started; a few coughs and it steadied up while the accelerator paddle was kept pressed and released a number of times. '*Bakki*', the 1961 Fiat was a dream come true. What was God up to?

Rain stopped, only clouds hovered, lifting up every moment. A rainbow came up in the direction of their destination. Kanwal gave more than what was decided for payment. His wife gave a one rupee coin and a packet of biscuits to a child in the lap of a village belle, who had been protecting him under a basket with a sack tied on top.

Going thereafter was smooth through thick jungles for almost 70 miles. There was hardly any village enroute and thus no people. Kanwal was in a dilemma that if the car had a mechanical problem, what would he do? He couldn't leave his family and go for help if required. Then the thought of dacoits came to his mind. He kept the loaded shotgun on his side and gave the revolver to his wife with instructions that if anybody tried to stop, 'shoot and shoot', to get through any trap. Nothing of that kind happened, except those frightfully high speed breakers, which were in abundance, to make up for the pits and craters of other Bihar roads. A herd of wild boars crossed the road. The thought of shooting them, despite being a keen and excellent hunter never occurred to Kanwal.

They were jolted out of their reverie, when the front right wheel got punctured just on the outskirts of Ranchi. A rickety shack was seen with a number of tyres piled up, as if waiting for them to arrive. Kanwal now understood the presence of some shining matter spread out on the road a few yards behind. Those were nails! What a game plan! It was getting dark and cold, and no time for some lousy argument. The puncture was fixed and they arrived at Ramgarh in an hour and half. Soaked luggage was removed by the men. The belated drink and dinner was a great welcome in a colleague's house. Their son was fast asleep since tired of witnessing his parents unnecessarily worrying about him. Their tale had reached the boss who sent a message asking Kanwal to take a day off the next day.

'Bakki' was given a great treat the next day of washing, cleaning, drying and polishing. But it wouldn't start, only gave out a whimper. The town mechanic took six days to put it back on an even keel. Kanwal borrowed from the civil contractor of his Unit to pay for *'Bakki's'* health to be ready to take on another adventure.

(For the sake of record, a huge number of people from Kanwal's family had learnt driving on the grey *'Bakki'*. It had met with 12 small and big accidents, was overhauled and painted five times during 17 years of caretaking by Kanwal and family. It had started giving 11 miles to a gallon, and ultimately left its family in turquoise blue, leaving Rupees 17,000 and that too without the carrier).

8

Come True: Soldier's Wishes

CHAUGACHA: THE SCRAMBLE

(Sketches 7 and 8 showing India-East Pakistan; and Battle of Chaugacha enclosed)

Millions of refugees from erstwhile East Bengal had poured into India as a result of genocide and atrocities committed by the Pakistan's government. It caused havoc in the adjoining states of India, especially West Bengal. A bitter decision had to be taken and thus to keep a check along the borders of any mischief by the Pakistanis or any effort of infiltration by their troops, Indian army was deployed along the border.

4 *Sikh*, relieved 1 JAK and was deployed to defend Boyra salient. It captured border outpost, Barni. Then on 17 November captured Makapur-Naodapara, about four kilometers deep into enemy territory and was thereby deployed at Makapur, Ballabhpur, Naodapara, Nayarpara and Hujli, almost six kilometers along a *bandh*. Many incidents of cross border firing, patrol skirmishes, bombing, counter attack and strafing by the enemy F-86 Sabers aircraft occurred. In their first sortie, the Sabers reconnoitered and threw smoke bombs for indication, in the second they bombed and rocketed and in the third they strafed. But because of being well entrenched, spread out and disciplined, there were no casualties inflicted on the troops except some civilians and their animals. The stench of blood was all over. In the evening of 19th November, a Squadron of 63 Cavalry married up with the Unit.

On 20th November, some civilians reported to Kanwal that enemy had vacated up to Sachandanga. Kanwal pleaded for exploitation of the opportunity. Permission was immediately granted to the Battalion to move and secure vacated areas.

The Battalion moved in three columns, on foot Kanwal's Company along the main road, Awasthy's cross-country and Duggal's along with Major Nishi Bal, the Second-in Command on tanks, remaining Battalion followed along the road. There was virtually a race, Kanwal reaching Mile 23 first and thus tasked to lean on river Kabadhak. Meanwhile Awasthy secured Purapara, and Duggal Khrincha. Because of some superb actions by Units of 9 Infantry Division, enemy had been forced to vacate forward positions and concentrate on more tactically-sound and essential positions, which included Chaugacha, a formidable defensive place astride Kabadhak river. Kanwal's Company moved along the most exposed and difficult route, the main road, and hence was subject to maximum enemy artillery and mortar fire.

Notwithstanding the enemy fire, several dozen civilians mostly ill-clad, with tears in their eyes, undernourished and weak, came from groves and villages around, touched the feet of the troops at the shout of, *"Joy Bangla"*. A few brought raw bananas or coconuts which had to be accepted lest they felt emotionally let down. The troops wanted to reciprocate but couldn't since there was hardly anything with them.

Duggal's Company that was mounted on tanks soon reached left of Kanwal's Company and they moved together for the last stretch of about a kilometer. The enemy was concentrated more on the river, astride the road. Their soldiers vacated west side of the bank, destroyed the only bridge in time to avoid its capture and occupied the bunkers on their home side bank which was made higher to dominate the attacker's side. They brought in a sustained machineguns fire and were able to inflict casualties on Kanwal's men by the time they were able to crawl to secure their side of the bank, moving from behind the trees and dig in. Duggal's troops occupied the area on the left. Attacker's machineguns, recoil-less guns and tanks started playing havoc upon the enemy. One of Indian T-55s was blown up in Kanwal's Company at the bridge area. Second Lieutenant Bhandari personally guided his tank forward and destroyed an enemy bunker.

Counter fire by both the sides continued the next day too, when on night 21-22 November, in a daring move the enemy crossed the river stealthily at a suitable place known to them and placed themselves on the right side of the road. It was at this juncture that Naib Subedar Nirmal Singh of Kanwal's Company with about 18 men launched a quick attack and uprooted the enemy, before they could create a difficult situation with their other troops on the counter move. A hand to hand fight was witnessed with full blast abuses from both the sides. Duggal with a platoon plus and Second-in Command with a troop of tanks moved in speedily to throw back the enemy.

Kanwal's Company had been fighting for the last four days. Nobody could rest. Kanwal himself was dead tired moving from trench to trench, exhorting men to do their best, which they did more than asked for. The Company thus was relieved to village Kangsaripur 2 km to the rear for some well earned rest. They dug up their trenches quickly. Two walls of an unfinished house were made use of to construct a makeshift bunker for Kanwal.

The Second in Command Major Bal of the Battalion came to visit. Somehow, he was always first to land up with the troops in contact with the enemy. They had their meal, took off their shoes and got into the small bunker, dirty smelling socks almost close to each other's nostrils and had just dozed off, when two Sabers attacked the *bandh* and the village where the Company was trying to get some respite.

Suddenly, the deafening sound pierced the ears of the two officers, the Sabers lowered themselves, and fired a salvo hitting the bunker, one bullet hitting inside just between Bal's face and Kanwal's feet, a plume of dust hit the former's face causing slight bruises and the bunker was filled with dust. Bal abused the pilots and got angry with Kanwal for getting a useless bunker made. Kanwal reminded him that with God's blessings three other bullets had hit the top and thus they were safe. Meanwhile two men were wounded badly.

Hardly had Bal washed his face when a thunderous sound was heard again and both the gentlemen ducked into the bunker at the same time that even the bunker quivered. They came out to hear a 'chattering' sound of three machine guns in anti aircraft role of Kanwal's Company, with tracers firing towards the sky, and soon a bailed out chair opened into a parachute just 150 metres away. A handsome Pakistani pilot Flying Lieutenant Parvez Q. Mehdi was apprehended, his pistol removed and he was about to be thrashed by the troops when Bal and Kanwal rescued him. The pilot confirmed the bullets from the ground had hit his aircraft. Another flash occurred and a thick black ball of smoke was seen a distance away, the second Saber having been downed by an Indian Gnat, the pilot died then and there.

Meanwhile, Duggal noticed a rickety country boat in the Kabadhak about a kilometer and half upstream. Orders were received that Duggal and Kanwal's troops will cross the river in shifts during the night 22-23rd and attack the enemy from the rear before dawn. Chahal's Company was moved further left to secure the flank. The crossing, though time-consuming and risky, was accomplished successfully. But somehow the enemy got wind of it and took to their heels in whatever transport they could muster. Awasthy's Company fetched up and thus Chaugacha was totally secured. Several trucks full of ammunition, equipment, personal belongings and rations were left behind by the enemy in a great hurry.

Sketch-7

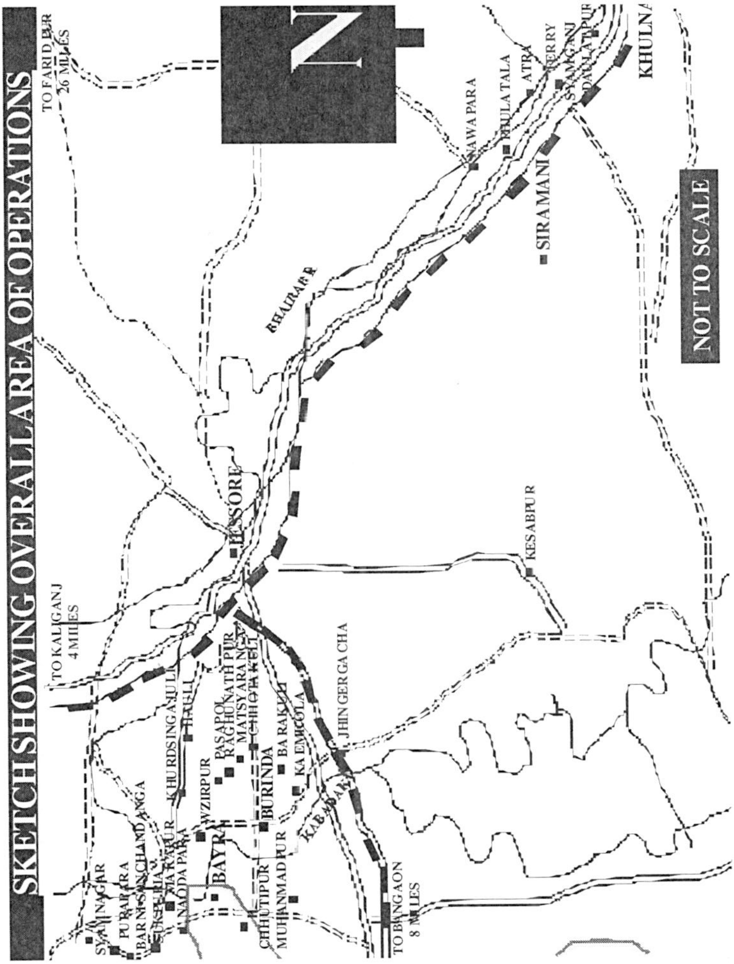
SKETCH SHOWING OVERALL AREA OF OPERATIONS
N
TO FARIDPUR 26 MILES
TO KALIGANJ 4 MILES
JESSORE
KESABPUR
JHINGERGACHA
NAWAPARA
FULTALA
ATRA
FERRY
DAULATPUR
KHULNA
SIRAMANI
NOT TO SCALE
BAYRA
BURINDA
CHHUTIPUR
MUHAMMADPUR
WZIRPUR
KHURDSINGA
PASAPOL
RAGHUNATH PUR
MATSYARANGA
BARAKULI
KAEMKOLA
TO BANGAON 8 MILES

Sketch-8 : Battle of Chaugacha

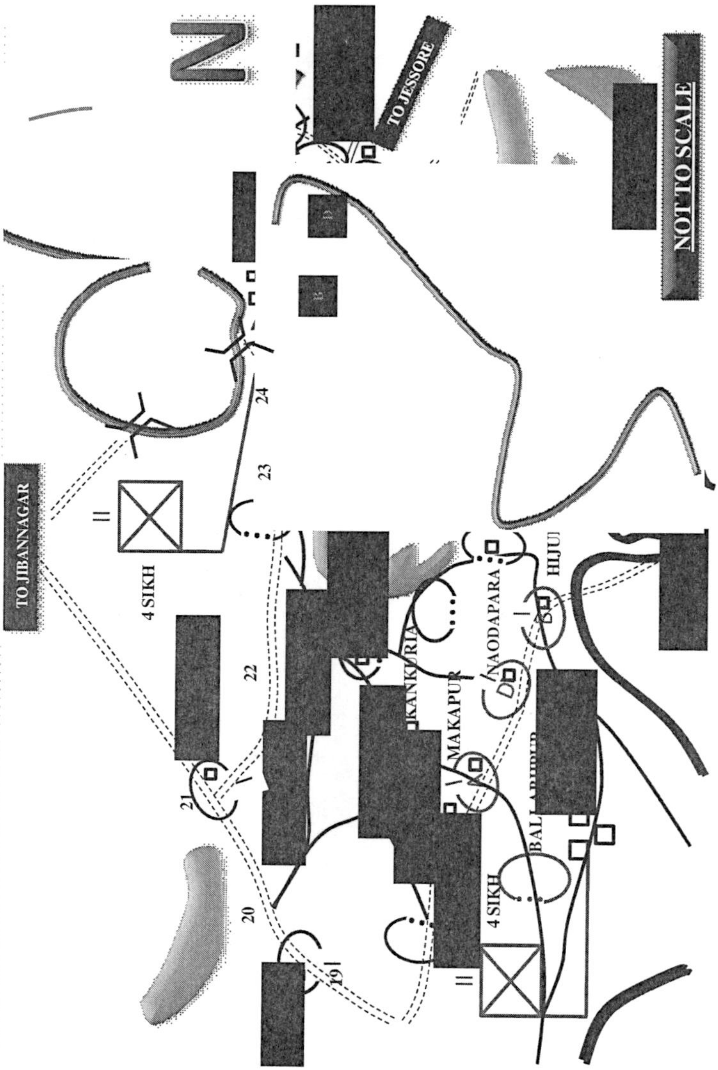

The American magazine 'Time' published news of Indian troops crossing in a blitzkrieg like movement which caused real escalation of hostilities. It was the deepest penetration so far. Meanwhile, another Battalion, 14 *Punjab* in a daring move had penetrated towards Garibpur further South-East and did a commendable job.

The Chaugacha winners were called back the very day they captured it to relieve a Unit at Boyra. While briefing the then Defense Minister at Boyra, the General Officer Commanding hailed the capture of Chaugacha and said, "This Unit was always ahead of everybody else by 24 hours." He further qualified the action as 'brilliant'. The Brigade Commander described it as a 'master stroke".

BURINDA-JESSORE: BIT BY BIT

The 1971 war was in full swing. Indian army's rightful onslaught into erstwhile East Pakistan was churning the Pakistani forces into a pulp. The super strategy of right time and methodology, meticulous planning, efficient preparations and bold execution was succeeding in every way. In the Jessore-Khulna Sector, with Chaugacha and Garibpur in the kitty, the battle was now raging towards Jessore. On the way there were some important pockets of resistance that needed to be captured.

At the outer defences of Jessore, the enemy had taken advantage of a two and half kilometers long *bandh* at Burinda and had deployed about 200 men under a brave, specially selected Major, in a series of bunkers, well stocked in ammunition and rations. Full advantage was taken of numerous ponds, narrow lanes in thick growth and mud houses in placing explosive slabs connected to trip wires; mines and booby traps were well planned and laid. Some of the bunkers were like mini-fortresses.

The overall defence system was based on villages Barakuli, Chhotakuli, Matsyranga, Burinda and Manoharpur. A mix of enemy troops deployed were from Pak 6 and 12 *Punjab* Battalions.

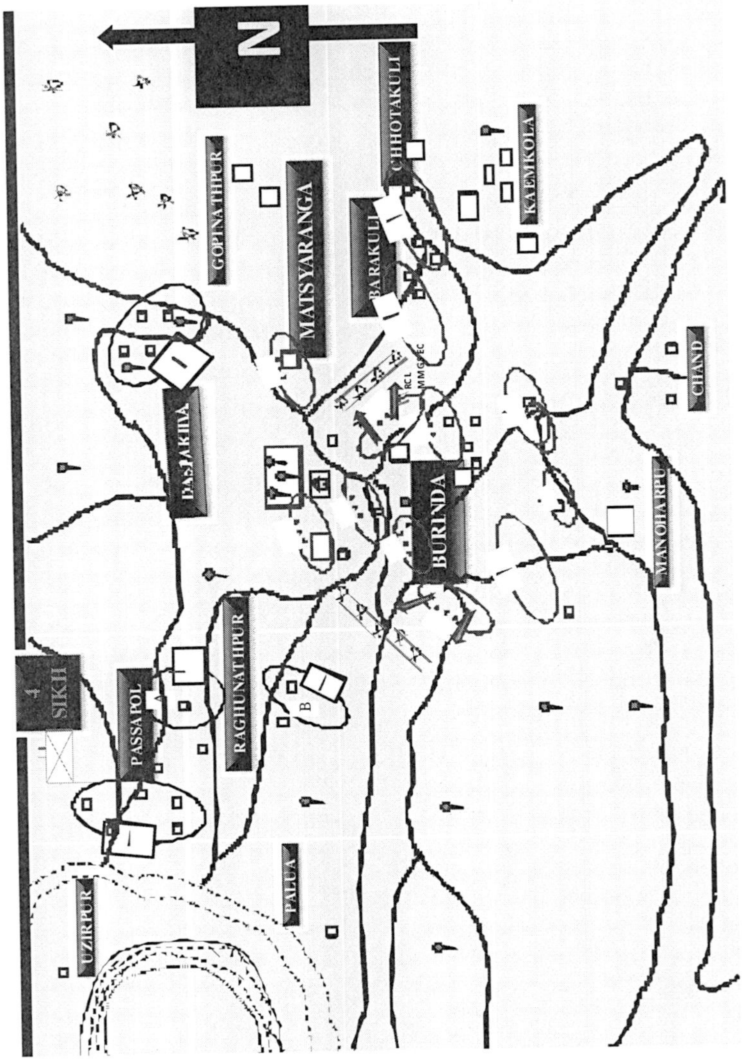

Sketch-9: Battle of Burinda

Sketch-9: Battle of Burinda

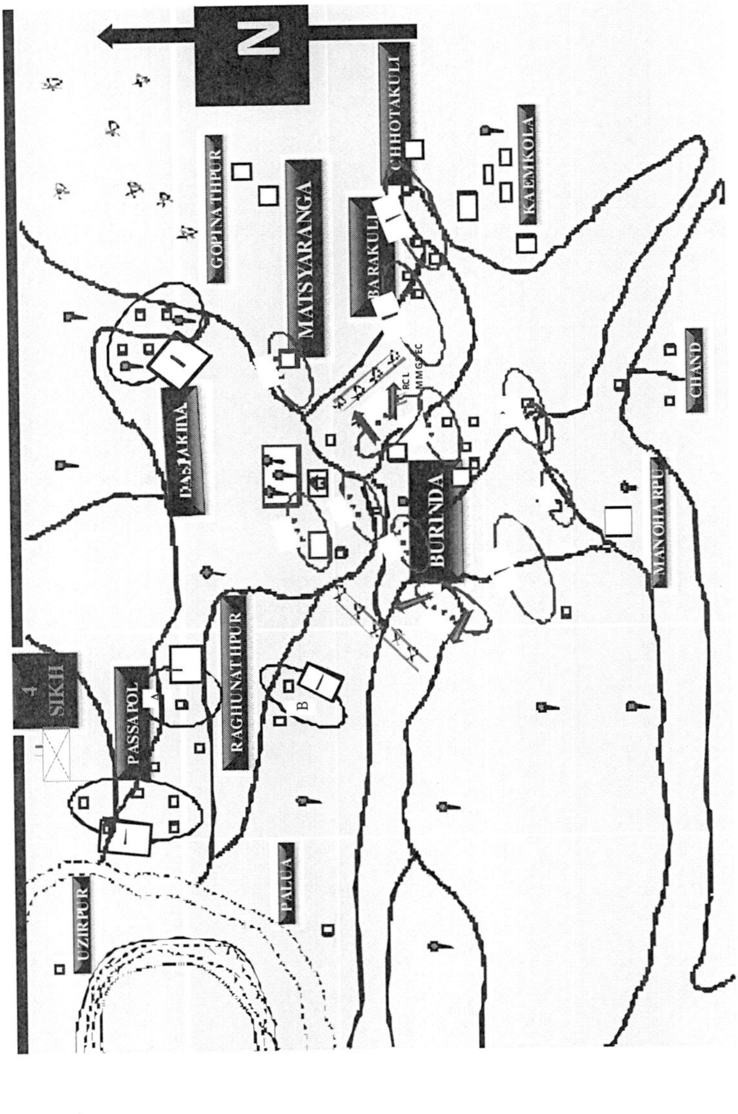

From 24 to 28 November, many minor and major adjustments took place in the Formation and units. Within 4 *Sikh,* Companies and Platoons moved to and fro, ultimately by 29th, Kanwal's 'D' was west of Passapol, the Battalion HQ at Passapol, Chahal's 'A' Company at Raghunathpur, Duggal's 'C' at Daspakhia, Awasthy's 'B' South-East of Passapol.

Courageous 1 JAK had attacked Burinda bravely but had not succeeded because of the tenacity and determined fight offered by the defenders. The Battalion had suffered heavy casualties. Ultimately, the task was given to 4 *Sikh*. The plan of attack had already been discussed with the higher headquarters. Earlier attacks had some weaknesses which were eradicated; support from armour and increased artillery punch was planned. The attack was to be frontal during day employing smoke screen.

The Commanding Officer discussed the plan with his senior officers. Kanwal, along with another Company was to attack in the first phase. Kanwal expressed his views that a frontal attack even with a smoke screen and supported by armoured shall be suicidal. He opined that maximum advantage of the information about the lie of the *bandh* be taken, it being elongated, and the attack should be from a flank, all four rifle Companies capturing bit by bit. The first Company's attack should be just after dusk. Before the launch of the first Company, as a deception plan, there should be frontal decoy movement of the tanks depicted with a full blast of firing by them and artillery, crescendo built up by the *'jaikaras'* by maximum troops available in front. With some reservations, the plan was accepted, especially when Kanwal volunteered to go first for the capture of Matsyaranga, which was at a limb of Burinda.

On the night of 30 November-1st December, the din of attack was worth hearing. The frontal attack was depicted in such reality by all that the enemy opened up with everything that they had in their arsenal. Meanwhile,

Kanwal's Company moved in attack formation from Daspakhia as stealthily as possible from the least expected flank and rear. After about 35 minutes move in the open ground by the Company, deception attack noises from the front were slowly stopped to give an impression to the enemy that they had foiled another attack. The decoy plan was at its best. Kanwal's Company, which was just about 40 yards from Matsyaranga, sprung a surprise, pounced upon the defenders with full throttled war cries and firing of hand held weapons.

The adversaries were in the process of loosening up for their food. About 20 of them were there, who were totally taken aback, picked up whatever weapons they could and bolted to the rear taking advantage of the dark and their knowledge of zigzag tracks through the thick foliage and host of trees. Some weapons, personal belongings and food were scattered all over. A pair of blood soaked khaki trousers and rags with red spots were seen behind the mosque, the tell tale marks of some wounded personnel.

The initial spectacular success paid rich dividends. As per the plan, two more Companies, one by one, were pressed under Chahal and Awasthy respectively, in a continuous assault, softening the enemy defences with fire. Due to enemy fire, Chahal's Company was a bit tardy in taking advantage of already bitten off limb of enemy's defenses and a day's valuable time was wasted. Commanding Officer Sidhu, then asked Kanwal personally to add on his Company's punch of fire of mortars and medium machine guns to assist Chahal to press on the further assault. This was done, and the enemy was made to repent for his stubborn fight.

Awasthy's Company moved up thereafter. Men pounced upon the enemy ferociously. Here, there was some leadership problem on part of the Company Commander and one of the Platoon Commanders due to which 11 soldiers were left dead in an area of eight square yards because of enemy's devastating fire. The men thereafter changed direction and captured the objective.

Duggal's Company, tanks following in mined area, moved to the other end of enemy defences from the rear. The few Pakistanis who were still lingering on to help the main body to escape were seen running for their lives.

A lot of war material was recovered. One of the documents seized was from the Pak Lieutenant Colonel Sham-Ul-Zaman of 12 *Punjab*, to Brigadier Hayat Khan, Commander, 107 Infantry Brigade, which was full of praises for courageous Major Hamid Ali, Second-in Command, Pak 12 *Punjab* who was commanding Burinda defences. 1 JAK who had attacked earlier was immediately informed to retrieve their martyrs whose bloated bodies were still in the minefields, 30 yards or so ahead of the *bandh*.

A '*mullan*' was captured by 'D' Company at Matsyaranga, hiding in the mosque. Kanwal saved him just in the nick of time to a bit of unhappiness of the troops. Next two days, the Battalion witnessed very accurate bombing by the enemy that must have been result of somebody hiding and guiding the fire. To his horror, his men exposed the *mullan*, the culprit, talking on a wireless set in a dug up portion inside the mosque.

Indian artillery fire was accurate and intense on his remaining positions for almost four days. Indian aircraft rocketed and bombed Barakuli, Chhotakuli and Kaemkola. They also used napalm bombs whose plumes of dust and smoke were well observed by Kanwal and his men.

The enemy was so unnerved by then that they abandoned the well prepared defences of Jessore without giving any fight, which was a mystery except that either they wanted to give a final consolidated fight at Khulna, or if possible, escape to West Pakistan by the sea route. Of course the brilliant offensive actions of the Indian forces had shaken them up and they were definitely in disarray.

Indian 7 *Punjab,* mounted on Armoured Personnel Carriers secured Jessore airfield on 7th December and maintained pressure on enemy. Pak soldiers' self structured myth of being the toughest troops in the world had exploded in their faces.

The ill-clad, under-nourished and devastated Bangladeshis came with presents of coconuts to express their gratitude. They narrated horrible stories of rapes, loot, atrocities and torture by the Pakistan's Army. They betrayed relief and satisfaction to witness the rout of their merciless marauders and perpetrators of '*shetanic*' deeds.

SIRAMANI-KHULNA: FASCINATING FINALE

(Sketch 10 showing battle enclosed)

Pakistan's Brigade comprising about five infantry battalions with matching other arms and services had acquitted reasonably well and finally withdrawn to their ultimate cocoon Khulna. Brigadier Hayat Khan was fighting a last ditch battle, independent of Jaffna-Dhaka forces. Enemy had deployed a strong screen position at Phultala, 17 kms North Khulna. Khulna had sea on two sides and Bhairav river on the third. The only direction from where India could attack was from the north, which was excellently defended, making use of the ground to its best advantage, even utilizing the huge industrial buildings which dominated the area in front besides providing protection. Mines had been laid; counter attacks assisted by armoured had been rehearsed. Stocking was mind boggling. Pak forces deployed were from 6 *Punjab*, 12 *Punjab, 15 FF,* 22 *FF and 21 Punjab (R&S),* The garrison thus was formidable and impregnable.

Attacks by 8 and 22 *Madras,* supported by armour from the northern direction could not make much headway. 1 JAK had earlier secured a narrow strip of 200 square meters along the Bhairav river after a fierce hand to hand battle. 13 *Dogra* had also launched an attack on Siramani west. It fell upon Dalip's Unit again to move along the Bhairav river in single line, get deployed in the small corridor of 200 square metres against promised 1000 square metres and launch an attack from the unexpected eastly direction; the road Jessore-Khulna as an objective 1,500 meters away, establish a road block, thus cutting off the enemy's forces into two, and then exploit further 500 meters to the railway line.

The attack was being planned by two Companies up in a conventional manner. Here Kanwal again suggested to the Commanding Officer that conventional attack would not take them up to even short of the road, not to say of reaching across the road, since the depth of the objective was too much. He suggested a Company by Company attack though of narrow front, as was done at Burinda. This was ultimately accepted.

On 16th evening, Awasthy's Company was launched first and thus achieved total surprise and was able to bite the first 500 meters with a determined fight against enemy's intense fire. By the time Duggal's Company was launched, enemy had got wind of this unexpected direction of attack and thus his one Company hastily readjusted their positions. Admiringly, Duggal's men attacked fiercely and despite casualties, captured their objective - another 500 meters. As his Company was in the process of digging in, enemy mounted a counter attack assisted by only one tank, a Chaffe, that they had in their kitty by now. A brave Havildar of Duggal's company knocked it out with an anti-tank grenade, which he fired from a distance of only 20 meters, his crawl of almost 100 meters remaining undetected.

The enemy by now had readjusted his position completely and also had moved into a couple of two or three storied industrial buildings that dominated the area effectively.

After midnight, Kanwal's Company started with fire and move tactics i.e., one Platoon of about 25 men on the ground while other group gave fire support, and the third remaining a little behind. Due to lack of time, enemy had scattered mines which could be seen and avoided. Enemy let loose hell and lit up the area with para flares. Kanwal ordered troops to lie down behind any bush, stone or wall they found and fire back. They were fortunate to find a small hut in which medium machineguns were deployed who started firing back.

The sound of the enemy fire was so intense that the Commanding Officer remarked, "Nothing will be left of this Company." He ordered Duggal to engage the enemy with whatever weapon he could. Kanwal requested for maximum possible artillery support which he got. Enemy started abusing in chosen language and Kanwal's men started replying. Each abuse of the attacker drew an accurate burst of fire from the enemy. Kanwal understood the ploy and told his men not to speak back and thus give away their position. This continued for more than two hours. Enemy fire though was immense but mostly non effective because of plunging fire from housetops, which was on fixed spots leaving maximum area safe. It was closing on to dawn. Kanwal had rearranged his fire support. Casualties were just three or four.

That is when with about 50 men; Kanwal attacked the last bit of 100 meters, almost running and entered an industrial building under construction. There was some resistance, but he captured nine Pakistani personnel, including a major with a lot of war material. The road was about 50 meters from there; positions were taken to bring any movement on road under fire. Scattered movement had started by enemy troops to the rear on fast vehicles. Kanwal's Company brought on heavy fire on the enemy trying to flee away.

Kanwal had been wounded the previous day by a shell and was advised by the doctor to be evacuated, but he had refused to go because of the final attack by the Unit. He had gone into the attack with the help of a stick and was virtually lifted from the injury side by a sturdy soldier. The same day Chahal was also wounded in his hand and had moved to the rear. Chahal's Company, now under Lieutenant Ahluwalia moved from Kanwal's location towards railway line. Hardly had he gone on to the road when he got a shell wound in his head. Kanwal had to rush his two men to bring him back as he was bleeding profusely. When offered water he indicated towards some more severely wounded men to be given water and evacuated first. While the brave soldiers were rushing to the railway track, Captain Gawaria, hardly knowing anybody in the Company, was sent to join it. He pressed forward and while firing on the enemy got a burst in his right hand. The task was completed.

There were about 22 dead bodies of enemy lying about. Kanwal asked a few of his men to get them collected for a respectful burial. Men hesitated initially, but soon got onto the job along with Pak prisoners of war.

By about nine in the morning on 17 Dec. our own major attack by infantry and tanks was in full swing. Suddenly, a jeep with four personnel, furling a white flag came from Khulna side. Kanwal ordered stopping of fire. A Pakistani Lieutenant Colonel, accompanied by a Subedar Major got down with their hands up, approached Kanwal and saluted. Kanwal shook hands with them. The Colonel expressed his Commander's desire for surrender.

The message was conveyed to Dalip who reached there in minutes. The Brigade Commander also fetched up in about half an hour. Meanwhile, the enemy Brigade Commander who already had been conveyed the message also came there. The Indian Commander first gave him a good dressing down and then soothed down a bit. The Indian General gave instructions for a formal surrender ceremony the next day. He also ordered that honour to enter Khulna shall go to Kanwal's Company. There was then a race. With own armour having arrived, Kanwal's Company mounted the tanks, with he himself on the first tank along with Major Gulati, the Squadron Commander.

The move to Khulna was rather slow because of thousands of Bangladeshis having swarmed the entire area with piercing slogans of '*Joy Bangla*'. They bowed with folded hands, waved, eyes moistened with happiness,

SKETCH-10: BATTLE OF SYAMGANJ AND SIRAMANI

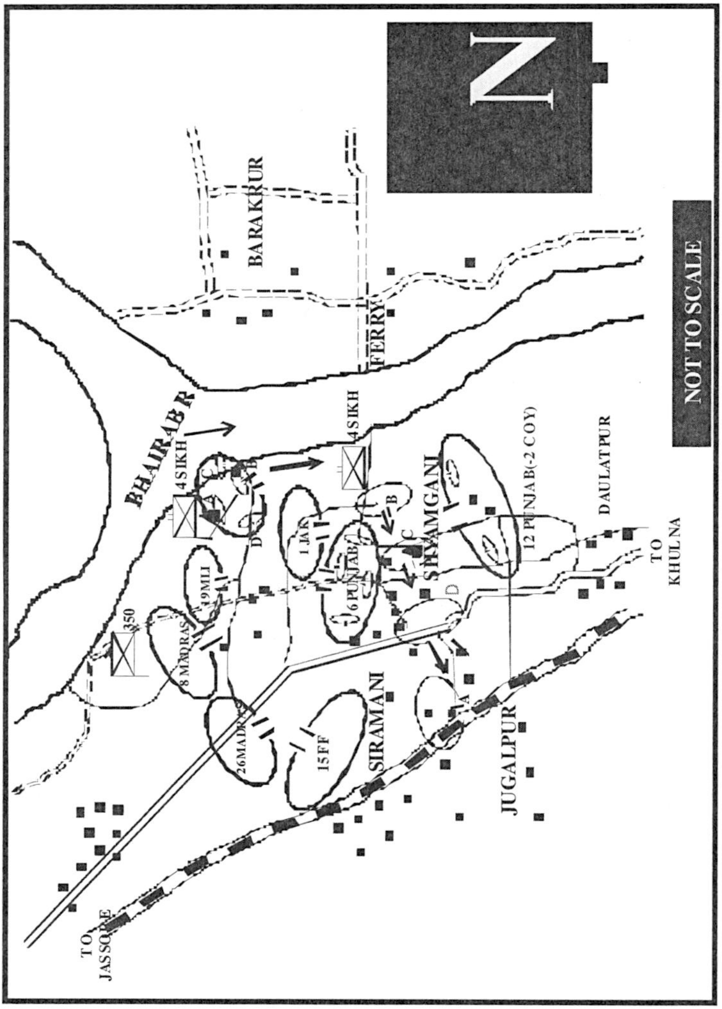

emotions surging and offering or throwing green leaves or few flowers that were available. Some held crudely stitched green flags with orange patches in the center – that for their National flag of an independent country. Happiness looked rather strange on their agonized weeping faces. There were few foreign cars with families outside or inside waving expressing their gratefulness. That was where Kanwal and Gulati saw a stunningly beautiful girl standing outside a car, waving at them. After a continuous hostile environment of nine months culminating into a month's war, the girl brought a feeling of homesickness.

Duggal had picked up an abandoned Toyata from somewhere and along with Kanwal witnessed the surrender ceremony the next day. The venue was full of hundreds of Indian army and air force personnel and thousands of civilians. The Pakistani Brigadier was marched to the sitting Indian General, the former saluted, laid his pistol and belt on the table and then his epaulets were cut. There was uproar of *'Joy Bangla'*.

PAKISTANI PRISONERS OF WAR

Responsibility to guard the Pakistani prisoners of war of their 1971 debacle in erstwhile East Pakistan was given at one of the camps to elite 4 *Sikh* at Ramgarh in Bihar. There were hundreds of prisoners including about 60 officers in the camp. Commander of Khulna garrison, Brigadier Hayat Khan was also imprisoned there, though in a separate accommodation. (The Sikh Regimental Centre is now located in the same accommodation). The Battalion was quite instrumental in the final fall of Khulna and had captured many.

It was interesting to note that these were the very barracks that had been built and used by the British Army to keep Japanese prisoners in World War II, and later also the Chinese prisoners — 30,000 strong of Chiang Kai Sheik's Army, who were pressed into advance against the Japanese in Burma.

All such stuff that could be used by the prisoners to escape was meticulously removed from the barracks. Care was taken to ensure that no such material was available that could be used to harm someone or himself. As per the Geneva Convention they were provided food of an Indian soldier. They were allowed out of the barracks in the open patches enclosed by barbed wire fence where they could exercise in the morning and play games in the evening. They were fully at liberty to follow their religious customs. They were rather comfortable compared to the unease of troops guarding them who were subject to all sorts of severities of weather—hot, humid and rainy, besides keeping tough vigil day and night.

In spite of all, there was an effort by the Pakistani soldiers to escape through a small gap left inadvertently in the fence. An alert Indian soldier emptied his self loading rifle's magazine of twenty rounds onto them from a distance of 30 yards, dropped five, other three running back to their barrack with their tails in their legs. Out of the five hit, one died the next day while others survived because of medical aid provided in a closeby hospital.

Not known why, but officer prisoners were allowed fans in their rooms where five of them were kept together. In one of the barracks there were nine officers in two rooms. After about three months, in one of the routine checks, when stepping up from the ground level to the verandah, Duggal found something amiss. He stepped back and inspected the ground closely. The ground was slightly soft in patches.

Also the level of ground and verandah was almost same. The prisoners were ordered out of their rooms, made to sit outside on the ground, guards around them and bayoneted rifles pointed at them. A thorough search was carried out of their belongings. Some trousers were found with holes in pockets and dirty with soil. The area outside was dug up. At one place two blades of ceiling fan were found buried in the ground. Inside the rooms, fans were put off and found to be short of a blade each. The amount of loose earth outside was mind boggling. From where had it come?

The prisoners were made to lie face down and given fulsome five hits of a stick each on their butts. The second round was to start when their senior Major agreed to tell what they had been up to. He was made to get up. He picked up a *'durrie'* (thick sheet spread under the bed) from under the accumulated earth, under which a tunnel had been dug up straight along the side of a huge cement pipe which had been made for the flow of soil of the half of the cantonment to a *nullah* in jungle to be drained into river Damodar. The tunnel thereafter was rounded off under the belly of the pipe and then ran under it for a few meters till outside the fence into the jungle. About 10 yards more of tunneling and it would have automatically emerged out in the slope in the open. The pipe provided protection against any caving in of earth.

One person dug, another passed on the soil above which others pocketed while doing exercise and then moved about throwing slowly, all trampling on it to solidify. The four feet diameter tunnel, 12 feet deep, 35 feet long under the sewerage pipe, and about 20 days of more effort would have taken the nine out in the jungle, then to Damodar, and then onto expected help from some locals for the realization of their escape. Their efforts had taken almost four months to accomplish this feat.

The ingenuity of the daredevilry of soldiers in captivity, an astoundingly superb plan, rare efficient execution and a will to survive with honour were their hallmarks. But then Duggal dashed all their plans to ground.

The boxing competition was after about four weeks. It was won hands down by the Battalion team trained on live target, morning and evening, thanks to the ingenuity of the Subedar Major, himself an earlier boxer. The prisoners, nine of them were in tatters, swollen and lost.

The trophy and numerous prizes that were won were shown to the prisoners who had tried to escape, their photographs taken and copies given to them. Alas, after repatriation they forgot what good they had done as yeoman service of working hard on the tunnel and then projecting themselves as live targets for the boxing team of the Battalion.

9

Hard Lessons

SQUANDERING SCOUNDRELS

The foothills in Arunachal, near Missamari, were famous for elephants. Several herds roamed about in jungles. They often moved into paddy fields mowing down acres. The military establishment was about 11 kilometers from Missamari. Some officers had their families residing close to the railway station and would daily go to their Units in organized transport or on their own two wheelers.

The bachelor officers staying in the Unit sometimes went to see a movie in the only cinema hall in the area of Missamari. On their return at night they often were confronted by elephants that shoved off when jeep horns were sounded along with blinking of lights. The road was a narrow tarmac with two yards wide green patches on both sides where the vehicles could cross each other; otherwise there was a two to three feet deep perpendicular cut downwards from where paddy fields started. The paddy fields extended to miles and miles, vast jungles thereafter and then hill ranges, hence the name to the area – 'Foothills'. Thus the elephants had hundreds of miles of area to themselves.

On one of such movie days when some officers, Kanwal, Partap, Hari, Virk and Dhaliwal were returning, and were just about two kilometers short of the Unit, they saw a rather big herd of elephants, about 20 of them, including three or four calves, standing, lying about or playing spread out on or along the road. The officers spotted them from a good eight hundred yards. They cautiously brought the jeep to 300 yards from the herd. The usual drill of honking of the horn and blinking of lights was resorted to, but the elephants wouldn't even budge from their positions. This carried on for over an hour.

Fortunately, the officers had some left-over whisky and were able to have a couple of shots more, to kill time. Two hours passed and some elephants got up and moved towards the jungle, but a few hundred yards and they returned to join those who had occupied the road and its vicinity. Seven or eight of them got into some kind of frenzy and started trampling the fields with funny and awkward movements. Three or four rolled in the fields, to get up, frolic, tease each other and in reaction hit each other. Officers witnessed this spectacular and rare sight admiringly. But soon they were hungry and irritated.

The honking and blinking was then mixed with angry shouts from the officers. This woke up elephants from their slumber. A couple of them started advancing towards the jeep. The heartbeats stopped and the driver was asked to turn about the jeep to escape. Somehow the elephants stopped moving forward, might be because of sharp light. The officers made plans to run away in case attacked but could not relish the idea of leaving the jeep. They felt that it was prudent not to further annoy the elephants. It was 3 am; another hour and it would soon be daylight, so they decided it was best to wait.

The elephants did move away in the wee-hours. Hungry, sleepy, bored and tired, the officers, without any drinks to kill some more time, reached their Unit at 4.30 am, and were totally aghast seeing a lot of activity in the Unit, particularly towards the canteens. The elephants had broken a shed and a wall of the liquor cellar, smashed most of the 100 boxes, consumed dozens of bottles where it was free for all and were 'glad' with mixed drinks, and had moved off. The mischief had taken just half an hour to occur, contrary to earlier couple of instances in other Units where they had enjoyed the forced hospitality for hours.

It was soon realized as to why the herd they were confronted with, conducted the way it did. Elephants also have the human trait of going berserk when drinks are mixed.

MIZORAM : BRIEFING

The Battalion had moved to Mizoram at the height of insurgency. The task was to guard the main road almost 200 kilometers long, from Silchar-Aizowal, the capital, to Zebouk and Lunglei. The deployment of the Battalion was in groups of 25 to 100 men on various posts. The Headquarters was in-between at Nathiala. Before the Unit was to be spread out, the Commander of the forces in the area, Brigadier Shamsher Singh VrC, an ex-CO of the Battalion, addressed the men.

People were most decent and docile. Not only were they innocent, but also were suave, well mannered and respectful. There was never a case of theft, and honesty so pronounced that people rarely locked their houses. They met all with smiles and warmth. They were religious to the core and all attended the Church services on Sunday. All invitees to a treat used to join the hosts working together to ensure the party to be a success, even to the extent of cleaning up after the meals. They valued their meager poultry that provided them eggs, an all important ingredient of their diet. A few orchids or some nice flowers like carnation, calendula and sunflower were often grown outside their huts or modest wood houses, built mostly on stilts.

They were fond of easy life, full of fun and frolic, dancing and singing. Youngsters were often seen with guitars around their necks which they played with finesse. They kept long hair, wore T-shirts with captions and tight fitting jeans. They also liked to wear caps. The girls kept their trimmed and flowing hair open or tied in a knot in the rear. Most looked pretty with fair complexion, features akin to Burmese or Chinese. They wore tight tops and loose *'lungis'*, a kind of cloth about one and half yards long, a yard wide, generally colourful, which they opened and tied frequently to tighten it around the hip with a quick flick of their apt hands. They were friendly and liked to socialize. The older folks did not interfere too much, except to guide, protect and shield, if required. Sometimes.

It used to be a matter of concern and difficult to comprehend as to how so many people had become violent to achieve their foreign-influenced-unscrupulous and misplaced aim for emancipation, when they had all that they wished for, while being a part of India.

To gain information about the insurgents, and to win hearts and minds of a sulking people, the army people, especially officers were allowed to visit their churches, schools or even their houses. As per their hospitable customs, the elderly introduced their families to the officers. A cup of *'thing poi'* (tea) was often offered, sometimes biscuits added. Where the relations improved, the officers took some presents, mostly in kind. Yes, whisky or rum was also offered which the locals relished. A seasoned local would generally ask the guests, "*no Nula rim?*" (*'nula'* meant girl and *'rim'*-enjoyment). But all this had to be within the realm of decency.

All especially remembered Commander's forceful personality and booming warning, "Socialsing will be kept within limits. Frequent opening of *lungis* and tightening shall not be taken as welcome indication. Their chicken shall be protected."

MIZORAM: CHHETLONG

The men of Chhetlong post had captured two insurgents from the jungles about 1,000 feet below their own picket at a height of about 4,000 feet. It was a chance catch. One insurgent had a country-made pistol that was available along the Burma border. He had seven rather longish cartridges on him, while the other insurgent had a bow and some arrows bound together with a shoe string, hidden in a bandolier. The arrows were made of resilient branches, split in front to accommodate deadly, sharpened and burnt bamboo shoots, tied tightly with bamboo peel. They both had hidden knives of about six-inch long blades and one of them had one crude type of grenade in a wooden cup, covered with uncooked rice.

They had red and yellow cloth pieces tied around their heads and some bird's feather stuck into them, the normal wear in Mizoram. They wore short tight shirts and *'lungis'* (colourful cloth), wrapped around tightly up to their knees, and rubber *chappals* with strings around the heels. Both had hollow bamboos hung around tightly, one had cooked rice and the other had water, tied on top with tarpaulin pieces. They were thus self-contained for at least a day. Both were stout, in 20s, eyes red due to the country liquor they had consumed in abundance, and were distressingly smelly and dirty.

They had bruises on arms, legs and faces they had suffered when they had tried to run away on seeing the troops. Had they not tried to run, the troops would have taken them to be some hunters as they more or less appeared to be so. They did get some kicks and controlled rifle butts on their haunches. Their hands were tied and were brought to the post.

The Company Commander, Partap, immediately on getting information on wireless, rang up Kanwal, the Officiating Commanding Officer, who was one-and-a-half hour drive away. Kanwal along with Virk, the Adjutant kicked off in no time. By the time they arrived at the post, the captives had been given water, tea and biscuits to put them at ease. They were moved to bunkers, separated, and then put to a barrage of questions by Virk, one by one. The interpreter was at hand. The essence of the questions was:

"From where were they coming and where were they going?"

"From where did they get their weapons?"

"Where did they get their training?"

"Who all were with them, how many and where were they?"

"What was their mission?"

After questioning politely with little information forthcoming, they were subjected to a bit of harsh treatment, again questioned, made to confront each other on conflicting statements, given some treatment and allowed time to think. Then Kanwal entered the arena and asked them to cooperate and that they would be taken care of. Some more information was revealed. Virk showed himself in the bunker and both bowed their heads on the ground and started blurting all that they knew.

Meanwhile, a posse of 20 men, fully armed to the teeth, with three days emergency rations, was ready outside. Interpreter and two friendly civilian guides were also in line. The captives were given medical aid and food. The whole process was completed in just three hours. Partap was to lead and his second was a seasoned mature Junior Commissioned Officer known for his business-like approach. The two insurgents were tied with ropes around their girth and hands tied with a nine-inch gap to balance themselves during speed march in mountainous jungles.

One insurgent in lead, couple of soldiers, guides, officer, the interpreter, second insurgent and the rest formed the line. They marched remaining couple of hours of daylight almost running and then marched as fast as they could throughout the night. The timings worked out perfectly right and they were pointed to a hut in thick patch of trees where the two captives were to join some others. The captives had told the officer that other insurgents were also to assemble there in twos and threes by the previous evening.

There was a water spring next to the hut which was so well camouflaged that could not be spotted easily. The hut was empty. Some smoldering twigs, goat bones, crumbs of cooked food and rice were strewn around. Couple of empty bamboo pieces reeking of country liquor were the tell tale marks of a party last night and breakfast early morning. They had then moved on to the final rendezvous for the ambush of a military convoy.

The strike was next morning at a selected spot where the road passed through narrow space dominated by unassailable hillocks. The captives, now fully cooperative, told them that there were nine people the group including themselves. The others had muskets, pistols, grenades and of course bows and arrows.

It was decided to move only a little more so as not to be spotted during day, rest at some secluded place with full precautions and move further well after dusk since the remaining distance was only a four-hour cautious walk at night.

The troops now rested, moved stealthily like a tiger, eyes wide open like a hawk and ears trained to hear the slightest of sounds like a wolf. There was three quarters of the moon shedding adequate light for the soldiers to be on some distance from each other while inching forward the last half a mile.

Good luck was in favour. The other seven insurgents were seen sleeping in an open patch after perhaps another bout of liquor, expecting no harm, having a nap as there were still three hours to daylight and keeping in mind the normal timings that the target would appear by lunch time only. Slowly and steadily, all seven were surrounded and nabbed even before they could open their eyes. Their weapons were confiscated, hands tied, blindfolded, led to the road, dumped in and tied to the same vehicles they were to destroy. They were taken to the Battalion Headquarters where a 'reception' awaited them.

10

Side Giggles

GOGGLES

Awkwardly framed, Kapoor was sprawled with limbs outstretched on a fairly steep climb during an exercise, holding nothing but dry leaves, clamouring for something to hold on to. Not succeeding, he started slipping downwards by millimeters huffing, producing funny gargling sounds, hissing and yelling: "save me, save me."

Kanwal quickly balanced himself on his feet, put his shoulder along the cliff and put both his hands under his slipping feet. Too heavy for a few moments, but Kanwal felt relieved looking up and seeing two men on their haunches bending downwards and holding Kapoor's hands firmly. Somehow Kapoor had abandoned all efforts to save himself shattered that he was. A couple of men took off their equipment and helping from sides, all five pulled and pushed Kapoor up to a safe place.

He lay down like a crocodile basking in the sun on sand along the river for a few minutes, yanked open his equipment and threw it away with the dirtiest of abuses. He said, "Thank you very much, I would have pulled up and climbed the hill but for the heavy pack that I was wearing which got stuck around my arms". Everyone was aware of his rather unbalanced physique and weak limbs. And his so-called heavy pack that carried only his night wears.

He had a small head with receding hairline, big ears, large nose on a relatively small face, roving eyes with scanty eye lashes, dark complexion, a large Adam's apple, small shoulders, large belly, larger bums and long dangling arms and legs. At six-feet-and-one-inch frame also, he carried a rather large pouch, so very revealing at the fly, no matter how baggy the tailor stitched the trousers. His jovial nature made him adorable.

Kapoor always bragged of his manliness and had stories to tell provided he got someone to listen to, and he never fell short of audience who were keen to listen to him, and later to mock at him behind his back. Sometimes, he did get suspicious of the way he got responses from his listeners but he told his stories enjoying this himself.

The officers decided to enjoy the good weather and planned a picnic. That day with his flashy red T-shirt, a brown belt on blue trousers, white socks, shining pointed brown shoes, a large steel bangle (*Kara* worn by Sikhs) on right hand wrist, a brimming smile, he came to the venue. He was wearing a new large golden-framed goggle which had dark brown glasses. He looked awesome and a formidable senior officer.

Below was a beautiful stream, gushing out of a gorge, upstream a ravine and then rich green mountains with most enchanting places like Kalimpong, Teesta, Darjeeling and Gangtok. The clear blue water was flowing under the bridge, gurgling, dancing, nursing the rocks, producing white lather, creating whirls and producing a humming sound – a kind of magical music on a windless sunny day, veiling the slight nip. It was one of the loveliest places selected for a picnic.

Kapoor was pleased to see the colour–eight officers, six ladies and eight children, including his own family. *Durries*, a few chairs, stools and tables had been arranged. The waiters had submerged a sack full of beer, sodas and cold drinks in cold water and tied it with a rope to a rock.

Some children along with young officers, and a couple of married ones, too, got into their shorts and swim gear and entered the stream, cursing the cold water, enjoying it and making themselves comfortable along the rocks next to the bank. The officers ensured that they were always downstream of the children. Ladies settled on rocks along the bank with their dainty feet into the water. A newly married was wearing silver anklets that were shining brightly.

Beer in bottles, juices in tumblers, and snacks-drumsticks and breast pieces were finished as quickly as presented. The going was as smooth and enjoyable as could be. Kapoor could not resist, changed into a pair of large short, wrapped himself in a towel, and with his goggles on, emerged from the tent, the change room, and entered the holy waters with a splash, only to stand up abruptly, almost abusing loudly, but restrained. His goggles were there, a couple of drops on the glasses, clouding his vision.

Mrs. D'Souza gestured to her husband and asked him, "Funny goggles! Why is he not removing them when in water?"

D'Souza, with all seriousness, "These are see-through glasses. He has specially got them from Bombay. Don't tell anyone."

Lady: "Now, what does that mean?"

Knowledgeable continued: "Haven't you heard about these new glasses, being used in USA and European countries at their airports to observe anybody's body carrying any objectionable object on person?"

Close by, the lady with the anklets remarked, "No, no, these must be for influenza."

The beautiful lady, moving her long eye lashes slowly, "Don't be stupid, let us get away from here. I should not have come here."

The stout one: "Let us throw water on him and drench his goggles completely."

The hush- hush talk was noticed by Mrs. Kapoor. She came closer to the other ladies and asked as to what was being discussed.

A bright one answered, "Madam, we are talking about real good weather today. A perfect day really! But we are finding the water too cold and we were thinking of moving to the chairs now." It was an excuse to get away from being gazed at by Kapoor.

A sudden flurry of loud sounds from the children– someone had caught a live fish in his cap.

Jerry looked towards Kanwal, Jitender, Ajit, SS and Jeeti who were listening to some escapade from Kapoor. Jerry was reminded of an earlier narrated story about Kapoor's encounter with a black lady. He looked towards Kapoor's pouch, hid under a dark thigh in shallow water, yet in its magnificence was evident with the raised fly of the wet shorts. His mind was lost in how the encounter would have been performed between the magnificent two.

Jerry was suddenly serious. He showed his intentional hesitance, avoiding any eye content with anybody and with a quiver in his voice, said, "Sir, did you hear today's news. Since air passengers are known for hiding expensive articles like gold biscuits, diamonds and revolvers in their inner clothes, the authorities in USA and European countries have issued see-through goggles to the selected staff to find illegal carriage of banned stuff."

Kapoor: "Quite possible, after all, science has advanced so much. We are into late 80s. Very soon, we will be having infra red goggles in our army to see intruders at night."

Ajit: "So sir, news about these goggles is true?"

Kapoor: "Yes, of course. Now boys shut up with your professional discussions. Don't you see ladies are already fed up with your talk and have moved away? Let us polish our entertainment skills, organize some game or dance on some Punjabi music."

It was immediately organized. Those in the water also had had enough of cold water and assembled for games and music. Somehow, Mrs. Kapoor came to know what was happening. She told her teenage daughter to get her father's goggles and hide them. Shwetta did so easily. Kapoor asked for his goggles many times, but 'no' as they had safely gone into his wife's purse, who somehow suppressed the urge to try them out.

Hidden laughs, smirking eyes looking sideways, gestures and low toned talks were all observed by Kapoor. He soon had put two and two together, taking away of his goggles and Jerry broaching the topic on see-through goggles. But any show of his anger or not being a part of the frolic would have made him a subject of ridicule, thus he played along superbly.

Next day, Jerry was called to Kapoor's office and thereafter was seen wearing the, by now famous, goggles and going about all the Companies. He had finished one round and he was on the second one. Other officers were hiding lest they came in front of Kapoor.

Kapoor called all stags to the Mess in the evening. He himself entered last, wearing goggles, with the announcement, "Now, I can finally distinguish between men and boys." The party was taken on by Kapoor as he was no more butt of the joke but the king of the day.

AN URGE

She was tall, well bestowed with feminine assets and curves. Her fair complexion and an ever-ready smile showed a glittering set of sparkling teeth peeping through fulsome red lips. She had high cheekbones which deceived of narrow eyes that really were not, particularly when armed with mascara. Long arms and legs with slim waist and well rounded behind made her desirable. Affectionate attitude and natural warmth compensated for slight high-headedness.

At 38, she looked gorgeous, be it in a sari or suit. She was very much wife of a handsome officer in a senior position. Married 12 years, the absence of a child was the only unhappiness they knew of. Doctors tested and treated both but fertility won't come by. Homeopaths used their formulae for prolonged durations but the desirous eluded. Soothsayers read the palms, applied their unfathomable banters and charms but to no results. Hindu, Sikh and Muslim priests tried their *'mantras'*, *'shabads'* and *'sooras'* respectively, along with all the rituals they could muster but of no use. Pilgrimages to religious places, and promises or vows to be fulfilled if got an offspring were all futile.

That streak of sadness and longing showed on her beautiful face, at parties, picnics, temple, watching or playing sports or cards, or even participating in dramatics which she was fond of. The married gents showered stealthy, and if possible, prolonged glimpses to see deep into the soul, shying away lest found out by their own spouses or the lingering fear of consequences of 'stealing affections of another's wife' or a missive in the annual confidential report and damage to a prospective career. The urge, however, was uncontrollable.

The empress had her own ways. She started showering her affections on bachelor officers. There were quite a few, each one endowed with a mix of handsomeness, humour, chivalry, beguiling respectfulness and innocence, and yet a burning desire. She danced with all. She loved their awkwardness for days and weeks till they were able to shed clumsiness. Rajni held special favours for Rahul.

It was a beautiful evening, cool and windless as can be in that historical town of Rajasthan. Sitting outside the club building, in the green immaculately mowed lawn, lined up with a variety of winter blooming flowers, *'raat ki rani'* with romantic fragrance and full moon transcended early February to make it the most enchanting month. The soft talk was disturbed by a fanciful uttering by an Assamese lady married to a Rajasthani creating a loud laughter that moved our Rajni's hand on Rahul's backhand as an innocent gesture of approval of an Assamese speaking Rajasthani. Rahul shivered to his bones and felt a quiver in his groins.

When Rahul sang that famous song of his in a melodious voice, glass in hand, his killing handsomeness, shy yet meaningful glances towards Rajni, she had her share of pounding of heart and a wave of weakness in the legs.

A tsunami was building up.

Rajni: "Rahul, how beautifully you sang! But why are you looking so lonesome?"

Rahul: "No Madam, I am, I, in fact..."

Rajni, almost in a whisper, "Listen handsome, you cannot hide from a woman. You are at the moment smitten with some urge. Is it love? Who is the lucky one?"

Rahul, taken aback, muttered, "But Madam, I haven't done anything of the sort."

Rajni: "I love your acting."

Rahul: "Madam, You are marvelous. I admire the way you carry everyone with you. What you felt about me I am not aware of. May I get a drink for you, Madam?"

Rajni: "Please do not fake. Don't be timid. I like to be with you."

Rahul: "Madam, you are so nice and helpful that all have feelings for you. In fact, I love your..."

Cutting his words, Rajni, with a weakening voice, "I want you, Rahul."

Rahul: "Madam, food has been laid. Wadhawan sir is also coming this side to request you for the same."

Rahul was no youngster any more. He was taut, he seethed, his heart thundered, he tossed about and did not have a single wink at night. When he was shaken out of his reverie with a cup of tea by his helper in the morning, he was anything but himself, sitting on a trampled wrinkled bed.

Rahul had grown up overnight. He had a resolve. He bolstered enough courage and sharp at 9 am, rang up his Rajni Madam, who picked up the receiver before the bell. Currents flew through the wires.

Rahul: "Good Morning, Madam."

Rajni: "Good morning, nice to hear the lonely boy."

Rahul: "Madam, I have been told that you are going to the market tomorrow to buy some stuff for the Mess, and I have been detailed to go along to assist in getting the desired official documentation done."

Rajni: "Yes, Jassi and Sarita are also coming."

Rahul: "Yes Madam, I will pick up both the ladies first and then come to you at 10 am. Will it be OK Madam?"

Rajni: imploring, "Yes, yes, but how have you been feeling since yesterday?"

Rahul, picking up courage, "Madam, frankly, I could not sleep throughout the night. Madam, I don't want to be late. I shall come to your place in time."

During shopping, followed by lunch in a restaurant, hands touched, shoulders and hips scratched, eyes gazed and lingered watching each other, mirth on lips shared and admiring gestures made. The day was short.

An entertainment programme was planned at the military station after a tactical exercise along the borders. The exercise was for three weeks. The responsibility for the entertainment programme was given to the Unit to which Rajni belonged. To help the ladies to supervise the various functions and entertainment programme, only a youngster could be spared, and who was better than Rahul, himself a singer and who took keen interest in event management. Rajni always reached the Mess 15-20 minutes earlier than other ladies, since her house was closest to the venue. Rahul, in any case, had to be present there earlier. Rajni could also afford to go later than others, who had to go to their homes to look after their children.

Kisses and embraces were stolen. Soon necessity and courage made them move to Rajni's place, Rahul always taking along or bringing back some book or something to do with the programme. Soon this necessity of an excuse also petered out.

The entertainment programme was a success.

There was also some glib acceptance by Rajni to a couple of ladies very close to her that her treatment by a famous gynecologist had been successful and that she had after all conceived. The confidential news spread like wild fire, some even congratulated her.

Peeping Toms and eaves-droppers, though careful lest caught in the act, did their best to get information on frequent meetings and utilized the knowledge as power. Rahul had become close to Rajni's husband and thus was welcome to their house any time. Since military transport was not easily available and the desert town's poor bus system was unsuitable, Rahul many a time offered to take Rajni on his scooter to the market.

What a happy twosome they had become! If she was exquisitely presentable and desirable, he was a tall, handsome man with a sweet voice and suave demeanor that could kill. Their closeness and mirth became an open secret and thus a subject of naughty whispers.

Enough was enough. Khorana, Sharma and Mangat got together. They had heard enough of nonsense. This dare-devilry was bringing a bad name. The joke had to be snubbed.

Khorana cornered Rahul. Seasoned that he was, he gave no chance to Rahul for denial, he narrated a few instances by date and time. Rahul was nervous, scared and apologetic.

Khorana: "Would you like to face an inquiry with military consequences or would you submit an apology to me to consider along with others to safeguard the honour of our Unit and that of the lady involved?"

A broken Rahul: “Sir, please advise me.”

Khorana: “OK, write down about your involvement and relationship, submit an apology and appeal for mercy. Come on; be quick before I change my mind.”

Rahul wrote down his acceptance of relationship and submitted for an apology. He touched Khorana’s feet, with tears in his eyes, and begged, “Please sir, save me. I am sorry for what I have done and I apologize. Sir, I request the honour of the lady be saved. I shall be indebted to you forever.” Khorana touched his moustache, kept his hand on Rahul’s shoulder and left. Rahul was standing in attention, head bowed and hands folded.

Rajni’s husband got wind of it. He discussed with Rahul’s boss. Rahul was sent on long leave. On return, he was parceled off to a three month course of instruction. Meanwhile, he got his posting orders to a staff appointment. Rajni’s husband also managed his posting as he couldn’t afford to stay in the heat of the desert. After a few years they adopted a child.

GOLF

At Sambha

Sambha, on way to Jammu from Pathankot, was a small township in broken area with small hillocks, perennial rivulets and a large one called Basantar in India and Degh in Pakistan. Sambha being only eight kilometers from the international border, was critical from the strategic point of view, hence an important location for adequate strength of troops.

Years back, somebody had designed a golf course in the helipad area, now abandoned, since rarely were golfers available there. It was a large ground, once used for football and athletics. Kanwal’s Unit reached there in 70s. He was keen to learn golf. He thus revived about seven holes, the so called ‘greens’ which actually were sand filled and thus the nomenclature, ‘brown’. To retain sand from flying off, used engine oil was mixed, which also made the surface smooth enough, for the run of the golf ball. Soon, a couple of old players and three freshers joined in. That made procurement of used engine oil easy from other Units. Recently posted Brigade Commander also expressed his desire to try his hand and God knows from where he dug out a golf set, all clubs mixed, in a completely worn out golf bag. Kanwal now felt relieved as his set was certainly a shade better than Commander's. Kanwal was his favourite to play with since he could beat him in two or three holes.

But not on that day. Three holes Kanwal had already won not by skill but by default, leading to the discomfort of the Commander. Kanwal was teeing off at the fourth one, praying that he went astray. The tee and the hole were diagonally opposite to the ground, across a road, further beyond scanty bushes, in a refreshingly green patch with a 'brown'. Distance was 340 yards and it was a par four. Kanwal could hit 220 yards. His tee off shot with a Mc Gregor wood that day carried about 210 yards, landed on the helipad 70 yards, onto road 40 yards, and ran on, not to be seen. Commander hit his usual, a little better, across the helipad, and well poised for his good second for a regulation hopefully, then a chip and a putt, roll and a putt or if the second shot on the brown then a putt and a putt, and if God willing just one putt for a birdie. The five-feet-four-inch Commander strutted forward, his fairest complexion and red lips showing the mirth for demolishing the foe ultimately.

The Commander played a dexterous hand and was on the brown, sure of a putt-putt thus a par. The caddies searched for Kanwal's ball and found it behind a rock. He thus took a drop by losing one stroke. Kanwal played the ball to a side sure of loss of hole but the golf ball had its own ways. It hit a stem of a bush, swerved towards the brown, hit the golf stick and was stuck up between the edge of the hole and the stick. The caddie took out the stick, ball dropped in. The caddie took out the ball and announced the ball to be *'sala-kanjar'*.

Kanwal: "Sir, I am playing with a Slazenger. I get a birdie."

Commander: "It beats all. Golf, eh! Let us apply for recognition of the course by Indian Golf Union. Damn the make '*Sala-Kanjar*'"

At Yeol

It looked so refreshingly green and amazingly luring – a nine-hole golf course at a height of about 4,000 feet. Surrounded by coniferous pine and teak trees, low hills and at a distance high snow-peaked Dhauladar ranges of Himachal Pradesh, with beautiful valleys and streams that added a godly charm. The April breeze was soothing and fragrant. There lingered a rustling sound of pine branches and leaves.

The highly serious war game of three days and nights had ended with splendid satisfaction of all the commanders. For those desirous to have a round of golf, or those like Kanwal detailed to play, there was a quick lunch. Of course a gala dinner was organized with entertainment and a sumptuous menu. Kanwal was to play in General's foursome, as chosen by the latter himself to revive the days of 1965-66 in the same Brigade, hunting sojourns and hockey and football matches when the General was a senior major and Kanwal a captain, both adjutants of their Battalions.

The tee-off, the foursome, General and a Brigadier on one side and another Brigadier and Kanwal on the other made the opposing teams. Others played a number five wood or a number three iron for a green at a distance of 190 yards. Kanwal took out his Mc Gregor three wood and made a jerky shot, 'looking up' before even 'reaching down' with his club, landing at the ball with a massive stroke, making it squeak to a large rock, about 50 yards away off the line to the right. The ball made a sound, striking at a caved in portion of the rock, bouncing back above the golfers, behind the 'tee', bounding like a rappeller and 400 yards down the slope.

"That is some golf", said the General through smiles, "a great hockey shot and the ball flying up and bouncing to the goal like football."

Kanwal, choked with laughter: "Sir that was for the good old days."

Brigadier: "The ball is out of bounds."

Kanwal: "Sir, May I play my second ball with penalty, of course?"

The evening party was full of giggles and gestures towards Kanwal. He relished all and was happy that he had become popular with loss of just one golf ball. He proved to one and all how well he played with the other.

At Tamilpur

The General, an excellent sportsman, was at that age, keen on golf and tennis. The golf course at Rangiya in Assam was only for namesake. So, the General would go to Tamilpur at least once a week. It took about 45 minutes one way. Tamilpur was a small town on the Indian side, a step short of Nepal, where Assamese and Nepalese lived happily. The Border Road Organization was committed to construct, repair, improve and maintain roads in Nepal. The movement across was open but restricted in those heady days of 1981-82.

The golf course was behind Commander's hut to which he referred as backyard. It was all small and big green patches, surrounded or interposed by groups of bamboo plantation, trees and a few hamlets where locals lived. On one side there were military barracks, well barricaded from the civil areas, minimizing the cases of venereal diseases. The golf fairways criss-crossed through, having fairly large openings as the golf course had been laid out ingeniously, letting the golfers play full zeal.

The General would always like to leave his Staff Officer Grade One at the headquarters at Rangiya while he was out. That day was an exception when he had come for an inspection for which he had to bring Kanwal along. Golf was fixed for the afternoon. Somehow, one of the golfers could not turn up; hence the axe fell upon Kanwal who was bestowed with a spare golf set from the Brigade and canvas shoes from the stores. While the military trousers were alright, a T-shirt fitted him well. Some bets had been laid though Kanwal had no idea in hell as to what was 'double' and 'redouble.' It was prudent to accept positively than betray ignorance. He always made maximum shots to reach a green and to his dismay he had to listen to conversation on par, birdie or bogey. He felt lucky if he lost a ball in out-of-bound area and fetched up to the next T-off directly.

On the seventh T-off, he hit a hook, sure the ball flying towards out-of-bounds area, when it hit a flying bird which dropped like a stone. The ball was corrected in its line of flight and landed a few yards ahead in the fairway. It was a real birdie for which Kanwal got ten points. The game continued, and remaining two holes were completed. The counting was done, the General's side winning the match but losing money to opponents due to the 'birdie' points scored by that fabulous shot by Kanwal.

At Nagrota

Just nine kilometers from Jammu, on way to Srinagar, nestled among hills and river Jammu Tavi, Nagrota a tiny township, was known more for stationing of Headquarters of a large military set up than for anything else. The Headquarters had as its head a Lieutenant General and number two a Major General, both extremely keen and seasoned golfers. Generally, they had to play with Colonels and Majors in their staff since none of the '*nav-rattans*' (nine jewels), that is, Brigadiers played the game at the time of this story.

The Lieutenant General and a Colonel were on one side and the Major General and a Major on the other. Halfway through the game, match still not decisive, they were playing the hole named 'Ass's Dropping', a three par, a distance of ninety yards, and a sheer drop in height from the 'tee' to the 'green'. The river was a few yards away from the 'green', and thus a shot ten yards ahead from the green meant loss of ball. A road made serpentine curves in between the 'tee' and 'green', dividing the distance in almost three equal sections. Major General was on the apron of the green, so pretty sure of a par. His partner was in between the green and the river in an uneven area, hence chances for a bogey that is holing out in four. The Lieutenant General was about fifteen yards to a side, with 50-50 chances for a par or a bogey.

Last to hit, Kanwal played a controlled number eight club, ball sliced towards the rocky area on the right, crossed out of bound line, hit a rock, ricocheted onto the higher portion of the road, jumped to the lower and rolled down the drop, gaining speed to cross half the green and rested four inches from the hole, poised for a certain birdie. The Major General did not like it and said, "Kanwal is out of reckoning since his ball has crossed into out of bound area and then bounced back."

The smiling Lieutenant General clarified, "No, I am sorry that is not so. The rule is unlike some other games. As per the Indian Golf Union rules, it is the final position of the ball which is counted."

Kanwal marked the ball since the Major General wanted him to earn his birdie by playing it. The Lieutenant General and the Major made 'one overs'. The Major General played a perfect roll, hit the pin, ball about eight inches from the hole, golf staff removed and he putted an easy par. Kanwal placed his ball, removed the marker, took stance and pushed the ball, which moved three inches and stopped suddenly. All shouted but with different reasons. Thereafter, Kanwal putted for a par.

When the senior General was away from ear's shot the junior General said, "There is always justice to IGU rules!"

At Miran Sahib (Jammu)

The annual golf match between the Northern Command and J&K Government teams was being played at the recently renovated golf course at Miran Sahib, a semi-hilly terrain, mostly along perennial Behlol Nala. Some water flowed in it even in non-rainy season. Three 'greens' were too close to the Nala. Golf balls, many a time, landed into a whirling portion of water.

The General Officer Commanding of the local Division, played the ball, sliced it landing into the whirlpool. The General played another ball. The match got over, awards were presented, spectacular lunch finished, and the guests started moving towards their transport. As the General stepped out, the JCO in-charge for maintenance of the golf course came panting with a satchel full of golf balls. The hefty Khalsa JCO, his fine moustache twirled up, proudly presented the satchel to the General and said, "Sir, Your golf ball that landed into the Behlol."

The General remarked, "Thank you Sahib, but I had lost only one."

The JCO of the Sikh Regiment, "No Sahib, all are yours; the earlier lost ones have also been found."

11

Treading Along

'KHALEEJ'

The flight was delayed by two hours since the weather department had not given clearance. The helicopter, a Cheetah, took off at 10 am with the Corps Commander and his Staff Officer, Kanwal, from Nagrota, for a very precariously constructed helipad at a pinnacle like piquet in Rajouri area in Jammu and Kashmir. The place was chosen as a venue for discussion for its dominance of area.

Just a few minutes from the piquet, weather packed up locally and became turbulent. In the squall, there were thick clouds dancing around the helicopter, reducing the visibility to a few yards. The ground could be seen only in patches; landmarks had to be recognized quickly to fly towards the destination. Air pockets were faced four or five times, helicopter dipping down suddenly, scaring the hell out of the passengers. Gusts of wind, heavy with clouds, hit the helicopter several times, wings taking a slant to balance and regain control, but with shattering and gurgling sounds hurting the ears. It was on the third attempt that the helipad was located with the help of smoke, wind direction registered from the fully upright fluttering wind sock; helicopter hovered and landed against lashing wind.

The passengers came out with cold breeze hitting their faces and making them shiver to their bones. They clutched the headgear the moment helicopter flew away, tearing their ears with a thundering sound and flying off bits of freshly snowed flakes.

The Division Commander was there to receive and lead to a view point in a glass house. Another General, two Brigadiers and four Colonels were already present. One of the Brigadiers took 45 minutes to brief about the landmarks, geography of the area, enemy positions, his likely objectives and modus operandi of infiltration and attack. He also briefed about the immediate problem of enemy infiltrating insurgents into the area.

Hot beverages during the tea break were a great welcome. The weather had also improved. Corps Commander came out to be shown three '*khaleej*' laid out by Kulwant, the Commanding Officer of the piquet area. An excellent hunter himself, the Corps Commander inquired how the three birds had been killed? Kulwant thought in Punjabi, translated to English, and thus took his time narrating the stories.

'*Khaleej*' was a jungle fowl found at a height between 4,000 to 7,000 feet above sea level. It was black in colour which shined. It had a red broad plume with matching flesh lobes hanging under its beak which was yellow. It had round dark brown eyes with a yellow shutter going up and down at necessary speed for alertness or relaxation. It had two or three yellowish brown feathers in both its wings and tail. The body was longish, well formed to give a cheetah like look. It had yellow long legs and broad feet with sharp nails. It was a sight to watch when it gave its melodious call, 'cock-a-doodle-do' with neck stretching upwards, neck feathers puffed up, wings slightly opened up and tail making a deliberate up and down movement.

Its spotting was difficult. Its fast speed flight was like an arrow. The bird was ever alert, swift on move and flight, and apt to go into a hide quickly. A hunter had to be sure footed, silent in tread, quick to shoot; lucky if he got it sitting on a branch or eating its picks from the ground, or finally a real good shot when the bird was in flight. The locals spotted its location from its crackle or droppings, and then hide in wait for the bird to appear to be shot with their muzzle loading gun or an arrow. They also used traps to catch it alive to be sold at a hefty price.

The discussion was resumed with all its seriousness; certain decisions were taken to redeploy some troops and modifications in tactics. Kanwal also gave his views that there was a need to train soldiers tactics of birds and animals, like a *'khaleej,'* appear innocent and an easy target to lure the infiltrator only to quickly disappear in a jiffy, be sharp witted and intelligent like an owl, quick to react and go for a kill with skills of a kingfisher and an eagle. There was a healthy laughter. The Division and Corps Commanders gave their closing comments.

It was sunny and bright, glass officers' mess was cozy and comfortable, chilled beer or brandy with hot water were cheering up the spirits with a variety of snacks. *'Khaleej'* took the cake with its unique flavour. The cook had done a marvelous job of marinating and cooking it in a *'handee,'* (earthen pitcher). Reports that weather was likely to pack up hastened the lunch. Helicopter arrived soon enough.

After a few days, an exercise was announced and was given the name *'Khaleej'*. The day tough exercise was over; a dinner party was laid out. A glass encasement was presented to the Corps Headquarters with a proud *'Khaleej'*, excellently and accurately stuffed, standing upright in all its glamour and royalty.

CONVINCING WAFFLE

It was one of the most immaculate sand model rooms. The model was correct to the last detail, with no difference left between the map and the actual on ground. Various colours used to show the actualities on ground – rivers, canals, trees, bushes, farms, huts, townships, tracks and roads were marvelously depicted. All the co-ordinates Northing, Easting, heights and distances were accurately marked. The model showed the international border and the line of control clearly.

Five syndicates of Blue Land forces (Indian) were seated in their groups, a little separately from each other. Each syndicate had five officers, one each from infantry, armoured and artillery, and others from any arm or service. All noticed that one of the syndicates had only four officers - the syndicate leader – a Brigadier missing. The only syndicate from Red Land forces (Pakistan) was seated on the opposite side. On the third neutral side were the Army Commander, three Corps Commanders and other senior officers, behind who were the observers. The fourth side was the General conducting the war game, behind who were large marked maps, enlargements, the screen, layouts etc.

There were also formation flags, enemy organization and few quotes of legends displayed. Outside security was elaborate and strict that even an insect could not enter the large arena and no outside sound could disturb the deliberations. The whole business looked very serious. Though overall there was a tremendous confidence among officers, but there was also a tinge of anxiety since the Army Commander had given a very serious warning that some people were not taking preparations for war as seriously as desired.

The business of discussion had started. Those present were tense, speakers being heard intensely, sand model seen minutely and minds working on how to compete with other syndicates and also annihilate the enemy's forces. All concentrated on each word said to fully comprehend its implication or interpretation.

Suddenly, one of the doors slowly opened, curtains parted and a figure started emerging. It was the indomitable Brigadier SS Singh, who entered; came to soundless attention and saluted. He tiptoed towards his seat as syndicate leader. The Army Commander thundered, "SS, you are late."

SS came to attention again, deliberated and said submissively, "Sir, Good Morning sir, I am sorry for being late. I was stuck in a terrible jam. I could have taken a risk but prudence prevailed. It is better to be late than being Late Brigadier SS Singh."

Pindrop silence. A few seconds later, a thunderous laughter by the Army Commander and almost simultaneously by all present.

Army Commander: "Come on SS, as always! Be seated."

The discussions resumed. Various plans of Blue Land were laid out. Red Land deployment was exposed. Rationales for attack were presented by the syndicates; questions asked and answered; critiques given and analyzed. A lot of data, though factual was bombarded, terrain, strategy and tactics possible were said; surprise and communication systems as force multipliers were propounded. Somehow, the Army Commander was not looking very satisfied. He looked at SS who had not uttered a word yet, "SS, are you dried up?"

SS spoke, "The attack plans are well-taken, understood and realized. These have minuses and pluses. There is no easy going. My syndicate has deliberated thread bare to present concrete plans to annihilate and subjugate the enemy. We have gone to the extent of analyzing the peculiarities of the enemy commander, his positive and negative traits, idiosyncrasies, likely reactions and responses to superior unpolluted minds of our commanders at the highest level. He is highly experienced, done a course each in USA and UK, fought the last war with us gallantly for which he was decorated. He is cunning in planning and merciless in execution. Gentlemen, the terrain being what it is, with its highs and lows, we shall put it to our best use. As I look at it, there are ample avenues to exploit provided we have the will and wherewithal which we have. Armour can be employed judiciously and vigorously. Our plans are precise to the minutest detail. Attack is a must. That's the only way to teach a lesson to the treacherous. Our coordinated, full velocity and meticulous dovetailing, particularly of artillery as we advance shall succeed. My syndicate's plans are thus hereby laid out. Sir, I have finished. If there are any questions to what I have said, I shall be too happy to reply."

After a pause of half a minute and no questions asked, the Army Commander said, "I have heard some worthwhile views since morning. I was, however, apprehensive we may not arrive at something concrete. I am happy to hear some factual and concrete plans as given by SS. I would like to hear something more specific and practical after the tea break."

In a corner, one Bengali Colonel Pal to a Punjabi Lieutenant Colonel Mandeep: "Yaar, what plans did Ass Ass Singh give for the Army Commander to appreciate so much?"

Mandeep: "Bullshit and harangue jumbled to perfection, and waffled eloquently with a gift of the gab. Obfuscate and confuse."

Madrasi: "Beat around the bush, blur the focus.

THREATS

Despite being advised to avoid taking over command of a Sikh Battalion second time in those turbulent times, after 1984 episode, Kanwal had accepted the challenge, especially since the purpose was to assist to win back the confidence of the politicians, bureaucrats and military brass, and also to reinstate the élan of the Regiment which had suffered because of problems created in some Units. Except for glib references, nobody had realized the necessity of educating the troops as to why there had to be a direct action at their most venerated religious place and thus to carry them along psychologically and emotionally. The thought of commanding a Sikh Unit in 1986 in Punjab was thus a nightmare to many.

After all, a 10-year insurgency resulting into a full fledged assault on the Golden Temple at Amritsar, assassination of one of the most popular prime ministers of the country, followed by terrible arson, loot, rape and gruesome murders, were more than enough for anyone to hesitate to command troops of the affected and aggrieved community. Kanwal, in any case, had no need to command a Unit second time from the career point of view. But the call of the duty was accentuated by the desire to command a Unit in which he was commissioned, had fought 1965 and 1971 wars, the Unit having been awarded 'Battle Honours' in both, and which had done exceedingly well fighting insurgencies.

The Unit was passing through a difficult phase. Fortunately, Kanwal's joining the Unit had an electrifying effect and the words of the Brigade Commander were, "There is a sea-change in the morale, pride and efficiency of the unit. Earlier men avoided seeing a senior officer and now were coming out to present themselves in their best."

But the positive approach, no-nonsense discipline, emphasis on hard work and a will to achieve spectacular results were not liked by some in the Unit, or perhaps some outsiders firing the shots from others' shoulders. Kanwal got his first anonymous letter, the essence being, "You watch out, you are going to be killed like General Vaidya, the previous Chief of the Army Staff who ordered attack on Golden Temple." After a few days, a second letter followed which said, "Rupees 5000/- have been given to 'people' with 10 cartridges to finish you." Kanwal divulged it only to his Subedar Major in total confidence with instruction to find out any disgruntled or mischievous person in the Unit itself.

After about a month, the Second in Command also received a threatening letter that he would be killed soon. He straightway spoke to someone who mattered, requesting to be posted out of the Unit immediately. Kanwal along with his wife visited his house, consoled him and his wife and convinced them that whosoever will come in his place shall also receive a same kind of letter, particularly if he was correct in his approach. Brave officers had to be in the

Unit and face any dire consequences. This threat could also be a hoax.

Just a week passed and the Adjutant of the Unit also received a threatening letter. The Adjutant was obedient to the system to its very best and a strict disciplinarian. The threat to him was that he along with his wife and two small daughters while crossing the canal on his scooter would be lifted and thrown into deep waters. When Kanwal along with his wife reached their house, he noted a very gloomy atmosphere. The Adjutant had asked for a transfer. Kanwal took a lot of time to convince him not to panic and stick to his duty, but fear in the minds of his family members persisted.

Kanwal ordered a special '*Sainik Sammelan*' the next morning. Besides some other points, he mentioned about the two letters that he had received. His address in substance was, "My life has been threatened. I feel proud that my name has been mentioned along with Gen. Vaidya, one of our most respected Chiefs. But I am unhappy that your Commanding Officer's price has been kept only at Rs. 5,000. Commanding Officer of this magnificent Unit certainly should be commanding much more than this paltry sum." The men started smiling.

Kanwal continued, "Also, why 10 cartridges? That means that the man chosen to kill is a doubtful shot." The smiles widened to grins.

He continued further, "I hope the killer knows that Kanwal shoots only flying partridges and ducks. I hope someone warns the killer." Some men laughed.

He added, "Two other officers have also received threatening letters. I want this to be stopped and thus I want my message to reach the 'detailed' killers. But I do not know how to convey this, through a letter, newspaper or radio? Since I am sure that none from my most dependable, courageous and patriotic Unit personnel shall ever be involved in such a cowardly act, I shall wait for another communication."

Never again did a threatening letter come to anyone thereafter.

THE 'KISS' FORMULA

A call from Colonel General Staff of the Divisional Headquarters directly to Kanwal, in command of the Battalion, for detailing him to prepare a presentation was a surprise, as normal procedure of following the channel through the Brigade had not been followed.

Jaggu: "Sir, good news, you have personally been named by the General Officer Commanding to prepare a presentation on newly inducted radars in our large defensive systems at Corps level against Pakistan."

Kanwal: "How come this task came directly to me and it may annoy my immediate boss."

Jaggu: "Not to worry sir, procedurally it will come to you through your Brigade Headquarters."

Kanwal: "But Jaggu, it is an artillery equipment; I being an infantry man will not understand it and shall not be able to do justice to the study."

Jaggu: "Sir, this was discussed, but the boss desires you to do it."

Kanwal immediately explained the matter to his Commander and requested for help as he was finding the equipment beyond his comprehension.

The Commander: "Kanwal, that is between you and the Division Headquarters. Don't involve me."

Kanwal discussed the present and the future equipment with the only Air Defense Major in the Division. He studied all the material available, raising numerous questions to understand the highly technical matter, simplifying it as much as he could and relate it to the prevailing strategic and tactical ground situation vis-à-vis the aerial attack capabilities of the adversary. His previous posting at the Corps Headquarters stood him in good stead.

With the help of maps, overlays and slides‘, the presentation was given to the General Officer Commanding, who said, “Hope we are on the correct lines. Improve it further and be ready to present it to the Corps Commander and other senior officers at the Corps Headquarters.”

The personnel at the Corps Headquarters were abuzz with lot of hush-hush talk during the tea break. Three presentations had been given, one by the General of a Division, one by a Gunner, Brigade Commander of an Infantry Brigade and one by the Commander of Corps Artillery Brigade. Only two were left, one of them being Kanwal's Division. Kanwal's boss asked the Corps Headquarters' senior staff officer as to how everything was going on because he was really apprehensive as other speakers were such senior officers as compared to Kanwal.

Brigadier General Staff: “Sir, bad, very bad. Lot of technical data of all sorts of equipment, comparisons and veracity has been bombarded. But hardly anything worthwhile has emerged in spite of questions from the Corps Commander and the Chief of Staff on strategic and tactical deployment. So far there is disappointment and annoyance.”

The General, feeling a bit low, gave a worried look to Kanwal,“So now, answers to strategic and tactical deployment?”

Kanwal: “Sir, I will try to answer questions as per your policy. In any case you are there, sir, to answer anything beyond me.”

The General, still concerned, uttered, “Yes, yes, of course.” And he moved away rather listlessly.

Meanwhile, Kanwal's charts had been fixed up. He further checked everything personally before all moved in. The Corps Commander whispered to the Chief of Staff and then murmured something to Kanwal's boss. Kanwal understood the vulnerability of an infantry Colonel. Wasting no time, he came to attention and asked for the permission to start.

He began the presentation, touching very little on technicalities, only drawing out the salient features of the new radar, evaluated the characteristics via-a-vis the old, crystallizing the strong and weak points as simply as possible in a broad manner that an Armoured Corps General known for quick grasp would like to know. Then he touched upon enemy aircraft, its likely lines of attack in relation to possible targets, area covered by the present radars, lacunae and suggested deployment of new radars, area coverage, protection, persistent weaknesses and remedial measures. He used several overlays on the Corps maps. It took 23 minutes against the allotted time of 45. Kanwal came to attention and said, "Sir, I have finished. Any clarifications I may have to give, Sir?"

Pin-drop silence for some time. No questions. The Corps Commander said, "This is the first sensible presentation making essentials clear for best utilization. Next presentation may be cancelled for the time being. Study teams comprising one Brigadier each from all the Divisions and Artillery Brigade Commander shall carry out further analysis and put up the final paper. Kanwal shall represent his Division."

During the lunch, Kanwal's boss, who was visibly excited for his presentation having been appreciated and accepted, told Kanwal, "You will come with me back to our place in the helicopter. My Aid-de-Cong shall bring your stuff by road."

Kanwal's hopes of a rendezvous with a bosom Brigadier friend enroute were dashed.

Learning of 'Keep it Simple, Stupid' (KISS) formula had once again worked well.

12

Responses

GUESTS IN INSURGENCY

The infiltration by the insurgents into J&K had started in real earnest in 1990s through Uri. The villages on both sides were very close to the temporary borders, and in some cases, almost adjoining. Comparatively, it was an easier area to infiltrate in the Valley. The heavy military presence was a deterrent to any civilian to cross over, but their deployment was primarily for protection of the line held against Pakistan's ill designs of military adventure. There was little intelligence available about training camps of insurgents, types of people enrolled, their aim and targets, their weapon and equipment system and tactics they were likely to adopt.

The first group of five infiltrators was intercepted about nine kilometers deep from the borders. Several AK-47s, pistols and hand grenades were recovered. This incident was followed by a number of operations in just three months time as the effort by Pakistan was to push in insurgents, as many as possible, during the summer month before the winters set in.

However, numerous actions taken in intelligence gaining, readjustment of positions on ground and additional stops and posts, were extremely effective. In this area, insurgents killed or apprehended, weapons and equipment recovered were colossal, almost as much as the total of remaining entire Valley and Rajouri-Poonch area put together by that time.

While infiltration became almost negligible in Uri area, it increased in tough terrain further North and South. But the visits of VVIPs and VIPs increased so much that the 'welcome' became a routine. Kanwal was fortunate to conduct Defense minister, Home Minister twice, three Governors who changed rather quickly, two Army Chiefs, Director Generals of Information Bureau, Police and BSF, to count a few. Apart from them, the Times magazine team and some press reporters also visited.

In fact, the VVIPs replaced insurgents necessitating a 'change in treatment'.

IDIOCIES

One

Uri Brigade Headquarters Education Officer was a bachelor Captain, who was dark to the core as far as his complexion was concerned and it had a shining texture since he applied the hair oil on his face too, which he used on his thickly-haired jet black growth on his absolutely round head. He had an equally dark large moustache. His collar bones and Adam's apple were always visible. His sparkling white teeth and eyes were the only digressions from the skin, which he showed out of the dress he wore. He was a Master of Arts in Geography and wanted to do it in History, too. He submitted an application to Bangalore University. The application was returned with some observations.

The joke went around that the requirement from the University was, "Your clearance of application is withheld for proper photograph in colour. X-ray won't do."

Two

The Education Officer had gone to south from where he purchased a high profile digital Canon, one of the best known cameras, to pursue his hobby. He had developed an enormous interest in photography. He had ample opportunity to satisfy his interest in enchanting locales of Uri. A good photographer was being arranged for the New Year eve. The young Captain convinced the officer responsible for photography coverage, to let him be the 'photographer' for the evening; more so to cover it cheaper and better; after all he possessed the finest camera of the time.

The Mess was beautifully decorated. Games and dances continued till the wee hours. All were satisfied that scores of photographs had been taken. The captain had suitably taken photographs from all angles, almost all bending down, kneeling or even sitting on his haunches, lengthwise or width-wise. The powerful flash had been on everybody and many times.

The positives were received from Baramulla having been developed and arranged in an album in the sequence these had been taken. The album was sent to all officers, under a note, "Price of each postcard size is Rs 5/. All the officers and ladies are requested to write their demand in the format attached. We are afraid all will have to recognize themselves from their 'behinds' and place their requirements."

THREE

Generalized discussions were going on among officers about various Infantry Regiments, the type of troops and their ways of life, and the greetings among troops. *Namaskar*, *Sat Sri Akal*, *Jai Durge*, *Jai Ram*, *Tagra raho* and *Ram Ram* etcetera were being discussed.

It was mentioned how Sikhs were fond of liquor, Dogras vegetables, Gurkhas of goats, Rajputs of chilly and Assamese birds and animals. Someone mentioned that Assamese from upper areas relished dogs, particularly black ones. Another enthusiastic one pointed out that the Assamese liked anything black.

A medical officer, from a field ambulance, who had the additional responsibility to visit the Assamese Unit everyday to see the sick, out-poured his worry, "I have a dark complexion, that is why, perhaps, they all keep on goading me with, *Tagra Raho, Sahib*."

MARCH TO INDIA

Insurgents started infiltrating from various routes when the insurgency was just establishing its roots in Jammu and Kashmir in 1989-90. The initial effort was to infiltrate through Uri area, along the old Mughal route from Muzafrabad-Chakothi in Pakistan Occupied Kashmir (POK) to Uri-Baramula-Srinagar in India along the river Jhelum. The ingress was on routes marked or unmarked, through most rough and rugged terrain, jungles or snow-covered mountains and then towards villages and towns. The same was the story towards Poonch-Rajouri. Soon, earlier considered easy ingress through Uri, had to be virtually abandoned by the infiltrators, due to extremely effective steps taken by the Indian Brigade, deployed there. The area became almost dormant while other sectors became active.

Pakistan resorted to another trick in this area and tried to augment its nefarious designs to depict to the world that Kashmiris of Azad Kashmir, as they like to call the POK, in thousands, were to move into India from Chakothi peacefully to claim part of Indian Kashmir. This audacity was unacceptable and rather looked foolish when there was so much of tension along the borders. Soldiers or civilians, nobody could even think of crossing over to the other side. Civilians in numbers crossing over, could lead to a tricky situation for the Indian government.

The line of control, at the road site, was along a *nullah*, with a 30 meter long steel wire rope bridge with wooden decking over it, called Kaman bridge later *Aman Setu.*. The ridge lines along the *nullah* were held by opposing sides. The bridge had five spans, three with India and two with POK. It was a partially demolished bridge. The stream under the bridge flowed into the river Jhelum 400 meters away. No four wheelers could move on the bridge because of broken wooden planks. UN officials often crossed over on foot to either side and used to have their meetings with their counterparts in POK or India. The Indian portion of the bridge was painted in tricolour, while POK side was green.

As the news got wings, the Indian Divisional Commander at Baramula conferred with Kanwal, the Commander at Uri and finalized their own responses to Pakistan's cunning plans. Kanwal visited the Kaman post immediately and fine-tuned each and every action to be carried out in an unprecedented event like this. The post had about 25 men under a matured officer who all were briefed to the minutest detail. All weapons were readied. A Couple of machine guns were added to cover the bridge effectively. Reinforcements were alerted to be employed in an emergency. A video camera and a still camera were suitably located so that each moment was captured. Troops, all along the border were warned to be extra alert for any kind of eventuality.

In the morning of 11th Feb, 1990, some people were noticed assembling at Chakothi, which was five kilometers from Kaman. The ruling clique had selected the day coinciding with the death anniversary of Maqbool Bhatt who was hanged for his crimes. Various people were seen making speeches while assembly became thicker and thicker each hour. By 3 pm, several hundred civilians were noticed, shouting slogans and waving hands and banners. Another hour and a half and they closed to 50 meters from Kaman.

Kanwal had by now moved to his operational room to control the situation in case of escalation. He was in constant touch with the Corps Commander at Srinagar, the Divisional Commander, and his Company Commander at Kaman. Minute to minute moves of the civilians, were being videotaped. They started moving closer to the bridge against blaring warnings on the loudspeakers that they should not cross the bridge otherwise they will be shot at despite being civilians. During this time, Pakistan posts fired several hundred rounds to divert attention and to build up pressure. Some civilians showed courage and started crossing the bridge.

Kanwal ordered the officer, Major Jasbir that warnings should be continued, and still if the civilians persisted, to fire two warning shots and if they stepped across the line of control, the Commander would be informed. The telephone line was through all the time, with the phones held to the ears.

Jasbir: "Sir, they have started crossing."

Kanwal ordered, "Fire."

Fourteen rounds were fired. Some Pakistanis dropped dead into the *nullah*, some jumped into it about 20 meters down and others ran back helter-skelter. On this information, Kanwal ordered a 'ceasefire' and to await further developments. But all was peaceful. The sun had slipped slowly below the horizon, the ranges resembled waves of an ocean in mid heave and there was an eerie silence all over.

The Corps Commander congratulated the Commander for handling well such a tricky situation. The Commander conveyed his deep appreciation to all of his command and especially the personnel who made it happen. After a while, the Divisional Commander rang up, "Kanwal, the Directors General Military Operations (DGMO) of both the countries have spoken on the Hot line and India has accepted Pakistan's request to allow their civilians to recover the bodies of their dead tomorrow morning. You plan how it is to be done? Then open your Hot line to your counterpart in POK and convey the modus operandi for the needful."

The hot line, generally kept dislocated at Kaman, was put through. With difficulty and prolonged effort Kanwal was able to get Pakistani Brigadier on line. Kanwal said, "Hello Brigadier, Good Evening, this is Brigadier from Uri speaking to you. Your DGMO has spoken to our DGMO requesting to allow your civilians to pick up the dead bodies of this afternoon's incident of your civilians crossing into Indian Territory. This has been accepted by our government."

The Pakistani Brigadier: "I am not aware of any talk between the two DGMOs. However, do let me know what has been decided."

A bit surprised that Pakistani Commander was ignorant to a matter of their concern; Kanwal replied, "You may please clarify this on your side. But I shall spell out the methodology to be followed to recover the bodies. At one time, three parties may be sent into the *nullah*, who if need be, can move into Indian side up to 20 meters or so. Each party shall comprise of four personnel. Each party shall have a white flag held upright to be visible to my troops lest they take it amiss and take appropriate action. The operation can start tomorrow at 9 am and must end by 5 pm."

Pakistani Commander: "Thank you; I shall come back to you on this."

There was no call till 11 am next day. The Divisional Commander said to Kanwal, "We have done our bit. No need for any further effort by our side to contact them. However, keep the Hot line open for one day more, that is, till tomorrow."

Whether the Pakistani civilians, who had jumped down into the *nullah* at the time of incident had picked up the bodies at that time only, or recovered at night or let some decompose or flow into Jhelum was not known. However, the British Broadcasting Radio, quoting POK PM Hayat Khan, announced that six personnel were killed and 14 others were injured. (That also was for excellent fire discipline and firing accuracy displayed by the Indian soldiers at Kaman).

This kind of incident was perhaps first ever after the Partition along the line of control. Pakistan hasn't tried such practice thereafter, realizing its failed consequences. (Except for one along the International Border at Jammu, where also they had failed to evoke any responses from the locals).

13

Buigle Calling

BABA JI

One

He was driving in Gurgaon. His wife was sitting next to him, strikingly beautiful with goggles on, looking rather young. He, though with his grey beard, looked elegant. The sudden red light as he had missed the yellow light because of a truck in front made him a culprit of traffic violation. A traffic policeman appeared from nowhere, stick in hand and whistle in his mouth. Kanwal had no choice; he slowed the car to the left of the road and stopped to notice the policeman almost breathing onto him. Watching the two inside, he said, "*Baba Ji*, be careful, don't jump the light. You can meet with an accident. Your young child is with you after all."

Kanwal was furious, he wanted to come out of car and argue with the constable as to how he distinguished between the ages. The lady laughed. Prudence prevailed. He moved the car with a grin and satisfaction how happy his wife was!

Two

Another one in Moga, in Punjab. The couple along with their children and grandchildren had gone for a movie. All entered the hall except Kanwal who went to the washroom. At the entrance to the hall, he told the guard that he was with a family who had just gone in. The guard promptly told the man with the torch, "Please hold hand of *Baba Ji* and guide him to his children, that big group that has just come."

Nevertheless, '*Baba*' remained stubborn and refused to colour his beard black and accepted to be the butt of the joke in the family.

Three

When 'Baba' was a young Colonel, his wife had been asked to participate in a show they named "Indian woman at her best." There were a number of young ladies who were taking part. They all were doing extremely well in some exquisitely rich attire to the great admiration of about 300-plus audience of officers and ladies. All showed off their dresses in the best manner tip-toeing to the tunes being played. Kanwal was sitting in the third row behind which some young officers were seated whom Kanwal did not know. Kanwal's wife appeared in a little bold dress and did her presentation. One of the officers behind Kanwal asked his friend, "*Oye yar*, who is she?" The other replied, "Not sure, but I think she is Colonel Kanwal's daughter."

Kanwal made it a point not to look back lest he was recognized and expressed 'congratulations' for his 'daughter' having done well in the fashion show.

LIGHT AND SOUND

A Reunion of the serving and retired personnel and a Biennial Conference of all the Commanding Officers, especially a Colour Presentation Parade thrown in with Chief of the Army Staff as chief guest, was an experience for Kanwal as Commandant of his Regimental Centre. Undeterred, enthusiastic and elated for being fortunate for shouldering such a responsibility, he set to do everything with élan. He remembered the magnificent Colour Presentation to a number of Battalions in 1966 at Meerut by the then President of India, Dr. Zakir Hussain, and of the spectacular parade in which he himself was one of the Contingent Commanders. He had also seen a Colour Presentation in his Centre at Ramgarh, Bihar, besides having attended five Biennial Conferences. He was fortunate to be at the helm of affairs on Centenary Celebrations of his Battalion in 1987. He was most fortunate to have the finest of personnel in the Centre. The support and guidance from all over was enormous and unending.

Apart from plethora of events decided, there was need for utmost planning, coordination, management of colossal resources, lots of practice and efficient execution for organizing depiction of Regimental history, through light and sound programme, which Kanwal decided to do, first time in the Centre. The so called '*panga*' was thus taken.

The event was planned in a recently upgraded stadium. The depiction included history from the start of Sikhism, birth of *Khalsa* as a race, rise of Banda Bahadur and *missals* (clans), kingship of Maharaja Ranjit Singh, the two wars with the British, raising of Sikh Battalions, their active participation in various battles in North-Western areas of Pakistan including the Battle of Saragarhi, the two world wars and numerous other battles that had led to the Regiment being the highest decorated in the Indian Army.

The script was finalized in a month; an audio was made, mostly being recorded by officers and ladies of the Regiment, with some help from TV artists of Ranchi. Hillocks and streams were created and arranged as mock ups to showcase battles. Horses and camels were arranged, uniforms of olden times as per the periods were procured or made, and hundreds of different lights for varied depictions were collected. Battle sounds to include war cries, firing by multitude of weapons to include guns, tanks and aircraft were recorded. Enormous screens, boards and placards were created, erected or laid on ground and hidden to be raised as per the event. Almost 400 officials including families and children were participating.

The rehearsals were done bit by bit, again and again, till some satisfaction, and then dovetailed into the complete picture. It was shaping up reasonably, but still far below expectations. Seven days to go before the D-day and Kanwal had to go out of station on official duty for three days.

Five days to the event and Kanwal got a call from his Deputy, Colonel Sain, that while other programmes were going on smoothly, the light and sound was not taking off. According to him the *'panga'* without any help from event management experts was falling apart and he recommended it to be scrapped from the programme. He further recommended that same could be substituted with a *'barakhana'* that was an evening with the troops. Kanwal thought for a while, and then said, "Hold on till I return tomorrow to see it myself. Meanwhile, continue the rehearsals and practices as scheduled." The Deputy understood that Commandant could not be dissuaded from the *'panga'* that he had undertaken. Thus, he took upon himself to do his utmost to make the event acceptable.

Kanwal returned to the Centre in the afternoon after about a 10-hour journey by train and straight went to the venue for a day-rehearsal. He noted the details and problems faced, and tided up for the night rehearsal. In the evening some flaws came to light. A rehearsal during the next day and one at night was carried out. Then a day was declared off as the guests had started arriving. Individual practices in their own groups were carried out. Verbal briefings by various event managers were done.

The final day. Hundreds of guests, including numerous VVIPs and VIPs were seated. Drinks were served. Kanwal gave the signal, dot on time, the programme started with a hymn by the Commandant's wife, followed by a one hour and fifteen minutes presentation. There was a pindrop silence. The eyes were popping out lest any detail was missed out, ears stretched, heart beats controlled, nerves lunging up and down, movements absolutely stand still, waiters with drinks and snacks shoo-shooed away by the gentry and the organizers keeping their fingers crossed, saw to the end of the event.

On the spur of the moment all stood up and gave a standing ovation. The applause was total and efforts of all had paid off; historical bonanza climaxing into a magnificent presentation had ended flawlessly. The *jaikaras* were astoundingly loud.

The Deputy hugged the Commandant again and again, with moist eyes and said, "Sir, our *'panga'* has delivered magnificently".

THE ROYALS

Brigadier Rathore was a scion of a royal family of a relatively small state in Rajasthan. He was hefty, tall and an awesome personality. His son was short, slim and drew no attention despite a huge moustache that he supported. In appearance the contrast was overwhelming. Brigadier was much larger than the Captain.

On the youngster's marriage, many erstwhile Royals were invited. The pack included Maharajas of Jaipur, Jodhpur, Kota, Dhen Kanal (Orissa) and King of Nepal, besides several others. There were of course some Army Officers, Kanwal being one of them.

A day before the marriage, for the 'ladies *sangeet*' almost all the guests had arrived. All were introduced to one another. Mostly royals around, Kanwal, too, was asked several times which State he belonged to. He soon picked up the idea to reply convincingly that he was not from any erstwhile empire but came from a family having some land in Punjab. There was no need for him to introduce himself, as the word floated around that he belonged to one of the prominent landlord families of Punjab. He was thanking his stars that at least all understood it to be Indian Punjab and not of Pakistan, known for the 22 richest ruling families. The initial embarrassment soon became reluctant acceptance, particularly under the influence of finest scotch.

'Ladies *sangeet*' was an exclusive affair. No gents, except very close relatives or real prominent people were permitted to be present where the elegant ladies, attired in royal ensembles of luxurious chiffons, their heads covered, sang songs or danced in most eloquent and majestic traditional steps. Kanwal was fortunate to be selected one of the close ones having a 'landlord' status and perhaps his wife's presence became a passport for consideration. Also present was a Colonel from Territorial Army whose military boss was Kanwal. The Colonel was the scion of the royal family from Dhen Kanal, who also happened to be a Minister of State in the Union Government. The wives of the two were mostly together, and furthermore generally were seen in the company of the Maharani of Nepal.

A number of 'smalls' of finest whiskeys were consumed by Kanwal, when he realized the impact of a mix of strong varied liquids. Something in his head jolted him and he told an officer close by to immediately lead him out to his car and then fetch his wife quickly for his speediest move back to the guest room.

The hangover next day was massive. He had to spend the day in the guest room only. Black coffee and plenty of juice with little food kept him intact. Only late in the evening, he could gather some senses to get ready for the marriage ceremony. They joined the procession enroute. The procession was a mass of decorated horses, camels and elephants on which were seated people with majestic dresses, turbans studded with jewels and diamonds and swords or scepters in their hands. The groom sat on an aristocratically decorated chair on the largest elephant. His moustache had been groomed to a twirl upwards. He was wearing a largish turban with a sapphire studded broach and a plume. Large size pearl necklaces hid portions of his red '*Shervani*', which had fine golden embroidery on the shoulders and cuffs. He looked majestic, large and handsome.

Not to mess up, Kanwal asked the driver to park the car at a suitable distance from the '*haveli*' of the bride's parents. The marriage procession was welcomed traditionally by playing *'nagaras'* and trumpets. Some rituals took place and all moved into the *'durbar hall'* kind of a large dome. The royals and guests sat in rows on a wide walk through with their swords in their hands, and huge studded rings adoring their fingers. The groom was sitting on a peacock throne in the center, on a raised pedestal.

Kanwal was made to sit somewhere in the center in the first row. Since attired only in a suit with his Regimental pin on the lapel, he sat erect to reach to some height of the Royals lest he be dwarfed. Somehow, he was looked after very well. His spontaneous smiles and appreciation of all had compensated for lack of Royalty.

Kanwals were lucky to see a spectacle they had only heard of or read in books. A dream come true, never repeated. But the news of murder of the family of King of Nepal afterwards was real sad since Kanwals had found them one of the most suave and gentle human beings, as the real Royals ought to be.

14

Capturing the Years

The seeds of growth sown by Late Dr Mohan Singh had fructified into a vast family line – spread in a number of towns and cities – almost all having done well in their fields of activity. They distinguished in medical, engineering, military, business and government jobs.

Surjit, the second eldest became a Brigadier in Remount Veterinary Services, died in harness due to brain hemorrhage, just when he was on the verge of completion of his farm house opposite Fazilka cantonment. His son Titu was at that time a Major in the Infantry. Titu was grievously wounded doing a heroic deed in Sri Lanka. It was a miracle he survived, and learnt later when in senses about the bravery award that had been bestowed upon him by a grateful Nation. He retired as a Colonel and lived in the house his father had built.

Baljit, the third in line, educated in London and Germany, decided to put up in Fazilka to look after the land, his father's clinic and his ailing parents. He later died in Australia due to a brain tumor which could not be treated for years. His son thus was a willy nilly custodian of all that was there, and lucky one at that because with time the land prices rocketed upwards phenomenally. The old house had started refusing repairs, and thus Reggie demolished it and made a new one at the same place.

Kanwal, the youngest, proposed to his elder brothers, to assemble at Fazilka for about two-three days.

Individually, they had been going there off and on. The eldest Sharanjit, a retired executive engineer, twice awarded by the Prime Minister for excellence in work; fourth in line Jagjit, an international famed neurologist, recipient of Padam Bhushan; and Professor Ranjit, a two-time awardee of Sahitiya awards by the Chief Ministers of Delhi for writing books — all came.

Sharanjit and Jagjit stayed with Titu at the farm house; Ranjit and Kanwal at the newly built house in Dr. Mohan Singh Street. Late Surjit's wife lived in her house with Titu. Late Baljit's wife had come to Reggie from Australia where she had become citizen of that country for the last decade.

The evening assembly was in the town house. Chairs, *mooras* and stools were all over. Glasses clinked. Jagjit, who rarely had a drink opted for wine, others for Chevas Regal, and ladies all sort of hot and cold beverages. Parduman, the eldest lady, wife of Sharanjit, looking at the newly built house, appreciated it, gushed, got emotional, and cried like a child, sobbed and said, "Where is my *Pita ji* and *Bhabo's* house?" Kanwal joked, "Gone with the wind."

Jagjit, in all seriousness said: "I had been wanting a museum of the old house where we could all have our memories chiseled." Amar, his wife said, "We wanted to contribute to the idea". Manpreet, Baljit's widow sobbed hard. Ranjit's wife Bholi kept her hand on her real sister Manpreet's hands, consoling, cooed something, which nobody heard, though all looked towards her.

Binnie, Kanwal's wife, totally composed, "Nobody can be like *Pita Ji* and *Bhabo*. I lived here for two years when Kanwal was in the field. They were just adorable. They gave me strength and solace. Look at it. My daughter, Sonam when one year old, swallowed something that got stuck in the throat. She choked, became yellow and blue when pointed out by Dixie (her son). Baljit Vir ji said "Quick to the hospital". Pita Ji, who was terribly sick rushed there. Bhabo, bed – ridden, with God's mercy, got up after four months, and moved to the hospital saying 'Meri bawa'. The treatment was successful" She made a face at Kanwal.

Remembering the glorious past, Sharanjit gave a dignified smile. Ranjit held his glass firmly and made a circular motion philosophically with the other hand. Titu took it to be 'universe is round'. Reggie thought '*Chacha*' was asking for another drink.

Kanwal narrated, 'One time *Bhapa Ji* Surjit, Ranjit and I had decided to build our houses on our land opposite cantonment area. Only *Bhapa Ji* made his house here. Well, that is how it is! Anyhow, here we are.' Nobody agreed or disagreed. Supreet, widow of Surjit, with a wholesome smile, gave her approval by moving her head 'up and down'.

The party warmed up. The ladies sang songs—Supreet her famous "*Zara rattan savere aa gorie, saanu tere milan da chaa gorie*", Binnie "*Lathe di chadar utte saleti rang mahia,*" Amar sang "*Kala doria kunde naal aria ee oe, ki chhota devera bhabee naal laria ee oe*". There was a charm all around of a joint-family look-like.

Titu said, "You get everything in Fazilka now, well cooked – be it chicken-*tandoori*, grilled, Chinese drumsticks; fish-Amritsari, roasted or fingers; mutton-*karahi* or *chaamps, kababs or dal-makhni*. Tomorrow we must try these". Ranjit remarked, "Hope it is not Fazilka dust-coated?" Reggie picked up his glass and without looking tried to sit on the *moorah* which slid, skidded and rolled away. Reggie tumbled, balanced at the edge of Titu's chair, allowing only a few drops of whisky to splash out of the glass. Kanwal and Titu gave out their beautiful number in husks, "*Cheecho-cheech ganerian, kitthe gaian khedan Channo terian te merian,*"—others' laughter not unabating.

Kanwal, a little abashed by a glum discussion, narrated the story of a drunkard. 'Natha went to a bar and asked the barman, "Please pour a large Black Label for me. I am very happy today. Offer a large one to all in the Bar on my account. And listen, one for you too". The barman happily complied. After a while, Natha commanded again, "I am indeed very happy today. Another large one for me, and same for all in the Bar and yourself." The barman again obliged. Natha now was in real good mood. He again blurted to the barman, "I am so happy. A 'Patiala' all-round." The barman warily asked for the payment at that moment. Natha said he had no money. The barman invited Natha to the room behind the Bar, gave him a good thrashing, took away his watch and golden ring, and kicked him out from the rear door. After a few minutes, the barman noticed the main door opening and found Natha toddling inside with a wavering gait, clothes dirty and torn, one eye black, a red smudge on the lower lip and dragging right foot in a broken sandal. The barman smiled to himself at his 'workmanship'. Natha to barman, "Aye, one large BL for me, and one each to all present here." The barman smiled and said mockingly, "Sir, how about me?" Natha looked at him disdainfully and said, "No. Not for you. Two drinks and you become quarrelsome."

The gathering had just finished laughing and in walked a little bald and bellied, thunderous Mr. Behal, "*Sat Sri Akal Bhapa Ji, Bharjai Ji* and *Bharao Bhaino*." He shook hand with all gents, embraced Kanwal, took his seat, and said, "I feel so proud to see entire family together. But Bahen Ji's family is not represented".

As he said this, Billu Bedi announced his arrival, rickshaw puller bringing in his suitcase. Billu represented family's eldest sister Manjit, who died a few years back. Billu looked a little haggard due to the long journey. Titu offered him his own glass. Billu examined the glass, took a sip and grimaced, perhaps not to his taste. Reggie poured a stiff one from the bottle. Behal thundered, "Long life Billu, we were just missing you. Long life to the family," and said 'cheers' with a cold drink.

Sharanjit inquired: "Behal, how is your business now?" Titu answered, "Daddy, his workshop is the biggest in the town, his restaurant is famous for food and he is getting the best land-produce." Behal to Kanwal : "I believe you had started export business, how is it doing?" Kanwal quipped: "*Bhara Ji*. Natha took franchise for Coca Cola to start his business in Saudi Arabia. He published huge posters and advertisements in magazines of repute. He showed picture of an undernourished Arabian, taking a sip of Coke, becoming larger, and then the third man taking the whole bottle emerging to be tall, muscular, handsome Arabian. Underneath, Natha wrote, 'Take Coca Cola, energy cum soothing drink.' After a couple of years, his friend Kartara met him and asked, "Nathia, you must be a tycoon by now". Natha replied, "No, business did not succeed. All the posters and magazines carrying our advertisements were mercilessly destroyed by the Arabians. Technical mistake has made me a pauper. The Arabians read the advertisement as per Urdu and Pushto, from right to left, from a strong man to a skinny beggar by drinking Coke. I saved my life hiding in broken Coke boxes till rescued by the police."

Manpreet announced, "Food is laid." Titu sensed the situation and rose to the occasion, "Ladies first, please." Reggie filled up the glasses for those wanting another one. Sharanjit gave an elder's smile and moved to the dining table. Billu helped himself with a Patiala and a largish chunk of food hungry that he was.

Next day, all had their bed tea at respective places and got over their morning essentials. By 11 am all were at Titu's place, all in Reggie's adjoining tube-well water tank. Reggie flew his mini-aircraft with great skill. Grilled quail, specially arranged from Agriculture University, Ludhiana, titillated taste buds. Fazilka's famous chicken-*tangris* and *paneer-pkauras* were a treat.

Setias from the town and Sardar Inder Singh's family from village Rampura joined in. Simple food of *aalu de pranthe, dahin-pakauri, maan-di-daal, kachumar-salad* and chicken pickle, were relished by all, admiring the taste to the satisfaction of Supreet. It was followed by ras-*malai* from famous Pakpatnias.

Binnie sang *"Saaki, chaman mein aake benakab ho, kalian bane surahian shabnam sharab ho."* Manpreet regaled with *"Pee le kisi ke bazam mein itna ki phir na utth sake, hosho hawaas kuchh nahin itne hein hoshiyar ham."* The afternoon siesta was a boon at respective places.

In the afternoon, Sharanjit, Jagjit and Ranjit visited biggest landlord of the town–Raja Ram, an old class-fellow of Late Surjit; and Surinder Ahuja, the most prominent entrepreneur, a close friend of Late Baljit. Luckily, Dr. Narula, the most successful doctor of the area was also present there. Billu accompanied Kanwal who visited his old class fellows–Trilochan, President of the Town Truck Union; Shivdev, an outstanding science teacher; and Rajinder, owner of accessories-cum-shoe-shop. Ladies spent their time in the '*choora* bazaar'.

Evening was again a get together. Dr. Bhopinder Singh, earlier Professor in Engineering College, Roorkie, came and narrated how he was endeavouring to rejuvenate the past glory of Fazilka, including efforts of the citizens to get a District status for the town. Motia *Massi,* our late mother's best friend came with the tastiest *kheer*. The tailor came with six of Binnie's Punjabi suits that he had stitched in one day. Billu was 'glad', never admitting like a seasoned *khilari,* telling his emotional stories when he studied in Fazilka.

Kanwal told the story. "Natha collected three bottles of country liquor. He opened the first one at first storey and consumed it; went up to the second storey and emptied the second one; not satisfied, climbed the third storey and knocked out the third one. He decided to bring more from the shopkeeper, missed the stairs, tripped from the roof without a railing, and fell to the ground with a bang. A lot of people collected all around. Someone sprinkled water on his face, which had no effect. A neighbour quickly brought some liquor and threw some drops on his mouth and nose. Natha revived in seconds. Someone asked him, "What happened?" Natha replied with surprise, "*Saanu ki pata, assi wi hune hi ayen aan.*" (No idea in hell; I have also just come).

Next morning, Jagjit and Kanwal moved off back to their towns, looking around longingly, yet satisfied. Sharanjit, Ranjit and Billu stayed another three days.

Fazilka was in the hearts and minds of all. They have tried to keep their parents alive in conscience, memory and deeds; the grand and grand-grand children of Dr. Mohan Singh and Amar Kaur adding to the excellence of line and warm roots of Fazilka.

Index